MOON MAGIC

Don't let its length fool you; this little book packs a powerful punch. As full as it could possibly be with useful information and practical activities, Pagan Portals Moon Magic provides a clear and direct interpretation of moon lore. Touching on a wide range of lunar-related subjects from moon-phase correspondences to astrology and Tarot, Rachel Patterson guides the reader through the practical aspects of rituals, spells and meditations based on the moon. The recipes for oils, incense and bath salts add depth and functionality to a book that is a quick read but that won't stay on the shelf for long; the person lucky enough to own a copy will page through it again and again for reference at every phase of the moon.

Laura Perry, author of *Ariadne's Thread: Awakening the Wonders of the Ancient Minoans in Our Modern Lives*

Moon Magic is a delightful treasury of lore and spiritual musings that should be essential to any planetary magic-worker's reading list.

David Salisbury, author of *The Deep Heart of Witchcraft*

Rachel Patterson has distilled the essence of everything connected with the moon into this wonderful and charming book. Moon phases, rituals, recipes, meditations, deities, power animals, signs, symbols, charms, spells, divination and so much more are tucked carefully within its pages and through it all shines the author's love of working with the moon and moon magic. A delight for everyone who gazes upon the moon and wonders how to work with its immense power

Yvonne Ryves, author of *Shaman Pathways Web of Life*

PAGAN PORTALS

Moon Magic

PAGAN PORTALS

Moon
Magic

Rachel Patterson

Winchester, UK
Washington, USA

First published by Moon Books, 2014
Moon Books is an imprint of John Hunt Publishing Ltd., Laurel House, Station Approach,
Alresford, Hants, SO24 9JH, UK
office1@jhpbooks.net
www.johnhuntpublishing.com
www.moon-books.net

For distributor details and how to order please visit the 'Ordering' section on our website.

ISBN: 978 1 78279 281 9

A CIP catalogue record for this book is available from the British Library.

Design: Stuart Davies
www.stuartdaviesart.com
Moon photograph: courtesy of NASA

Printed and bound by CPI Group (UK) Ltd, Croydon, CR0 4YY

We operate a distinctive and ethical publishing philosophy in all
areas of our business, from our global network of authors to
production and worldwide distribution.

CONTENTS

Who Am I?

My craft name is Tansy Firedragon and I have been a witch for many years now. I have studied many areas of the Craft utilising books, online resources, schools and from studying with some wonderful mentors such as Janet Farrar and Gavin Bone. I have worked through the first, second and third Wiccan Degrees. Pagan Portals Moon Magic is my fourth published book with Moon Books.

I am High Priestess in my own coven co run by my lovely sisters in the craft, The Kitchen Witch Coven of Natural Witchery, which allows me to attend lots of outside rituals in wonderful sacred places within the UK. We also run workshops locally.

My website: www.rachelpatterson.co.uk

My personal blog: www.tansyfiredragon.blogspot.co.uk

Email: tansyfiredragon@yahoo.com

I am co-founder and a leadership team member of the online Kitchen Witch School of Natural Witchcraft; we also have a facebook page and a blog.

www.kitchenwitchhearth.com

www.kitchenwitchhearth.wix.com/coven

www.kitchenwitchuk.blogspot.co.uk

www.facebook.com/kitchenwitchuk

My craft is a combination of old religion witchcraft, Wicca, kitchen witchery, green witchery and hoodoo. My heart is that of a Kitchen Witch. I am blessed with a wonderful husband and I thank him for all his support, lovely children, a fabulous family and good friends. A special thanks also to my sisters in the Craft, Tracey and Lesley, for being the best friends a Witch could ever need. Thank you to Lesley for writing not only the opening poem in this book, but also sharing her version of the Charge of the Goddess.

The Moon

A poem by Lesley Lightbody
Silvery light from the bright full Moon
Shining down, illuminates the room
Goddess in her Mother guise
Shines like a beacon in the skies

Soft the light shining from above
Like the wings on a pure white dove
Filled with hope and promise to come
Silvery light brings me home

Waxing, Waning, Full or New
The Goddess shines upon me and you
Illuminating our Path so bright
Follow the Moon and all is right

The Moon: Introduction

The Moon is such a beautiful sight in our skies; she is full of mystery and intrigue yet also full of immense power. She has been seen through history as being part of the occult and linked to enchanters, magicians and witches alike. Images abound of a wolf howling to the Moon and of witches flying on broomsticks silhouetted against her as a backdrop.

She is a huge part of all sorts of pagan pathways and plays a very important role in all areas of working magic.

Observing and working with the Moon and her phases is one of the ways we can tune into the here and now and the universe that surrounds us, learning to go with the flow of energy and follow her course. Working with the phases of the Moon also helps us to understand our own body and our inner thoughts, feelings and emotions. She controls the tides of the oceans; so the Moon is very much about our emotions which are linked to the element of water.

Within this book I hope to open up some of the mystery and guide you through working with her phases and to tap into her powerful energy.

We will start with the basics of the lunar cycle, the representations and correspondences of each phase, what magic to work and when. We will also take a look at the lunar year, Moon deities, Moon spells, meditations, specific Moon rituals, Moon names, tree Moons and Moon recipes.

Before performing spells and rites, it is a good idea to meditate about what you are trying to achieve and how. The phase of the Moon is something on which to reflect. Things can always be adapted – for instance a healing spell with a Waning Moon could concentrate on banishing the illness, whereas with a Waxing Moon it would be better to visualize increasing well-being.

I have purposely kept the wording within the rituals simple, but you can add your own words, deities and blessings to personalise them, they just give you a framework upon which to start.

There are several spells within this book, you can use them as they are or use your own instinct and intuition to tweak them to suit you, add your own personal twist to them. With all spell work the important part is your intent. Good visualisation, clear instructions and focus will all help to make your spell powerful. Please be very careful with your wording and your wishes, make sure you have stated your intent with great clarity as spells have a habit of working in extremely unexpected ways.

Please be careful when working with essential oils, always do a skin check. If you are pregnant my advice would be to avoid using oils totally unless you seek specialist advice.

Esbats

The word 'esbat' is believed to be derived from a French word *s'esbattre* which means to 'joyfully celebrate' and is actually quite fitting. The term esbat is usually used now to mean a coming together of like-minded people to celebrate the phases of the Moon with a ritual and/or spell work. It doesn't have to be on a Full Moon or New Moon, it can be for any of the phases of the Moon or planetary alignments and may involve teaching, lessons or training of some sort as well.

The Lunar Cycle

Firstly we need to understand the basics of the lunar cycle so here is the technical bit:

The Moon has several cycles, but the one that is the most obvious and that concerns us principally is that of the Moon's phases.

The light of the Moon is reflected from the Sun. Although from a more subtle perspective it is evident that moonlight has its own special properties, the Moon herself has no luminescence.

The phases of the Moon are caused by the light of the Sun being reflected in a different way, owing to the changing relationship between Earth, Moon and Sun.

The phases of the Moon are the same all over the Earth. When it is a Full Moon in Britain it is also a Full Moon in Australia, China and the United States.

The passage of the Moon from New Moon to New Moon takes 29½ days. This phase cycle is called the synodic month, but this can vary by as much as 13 hours because of the eccentricity of the Moon's orbit around the Earth.

As there are 365 days in the year, most years have 13 New Moons or 13 Full Moons, but never both. Occasionally a year will miss out and only have 12 of each.

The lunar cycle can be divided and subdivided in a variety of ways because it's a cycle, and the different parts of the cycle naturally blend.

The usual way of considering the lunar cycle is to divide it into four – New Moon, Waxing Moon, Full Moon and Waning Moon – or eight with the addition of the Waning Crescent (or Balsamic), the Waning Gibbous (or Disseminating), Waxing Gibbous and Waxing Crescent Moons.

Within these parts there is continual variation, as the energies involved are perpetually on the move, growing and decreasing.

Why do we try to correspond our workings to the phases of the Moon? It is because corresponding magical workings to the phase of the Moon will add more power to them.

New Moon

We consider it to be the New Moon up to 3½ days after the official New Moon. She rises around dawn, sets around sunset. Because she is between the Sun and the Earth nothing or very little is reflected and for a few days the Moon is lost in the brilliance of the Sun. When we cannot see any Moon in the sky, after the Waning Moon and before we see the first glimpse of the Crescent it is often referred to as the Dark Moon (see further chapter for more details).

As the Sun and Moon are on the same side of the Earth, the pull on us is the strongest. Because the Sun, Moon and Earth are all in a straight line this creates a time when the high tide is higher and the low tide is lower than usual.

This is a wonderful time to make new beginnings of all types. It is especially good for getting rid of bad habits. Habitual ways of thinking that are harmful and negative can also be abandoned at this time. It is also a good time to start something creative. New projects at work can also be launched.

The first day of the New Moon is really best devoted to the planning stages of ventures. It is good to feel just a little excited and filled with anticipation, although your energy may not be at its highest. A day or two into the cycle is the time to take the initiative, apply for that job, and start house hunting or any similar endeavours. It is also good for attracting positive energies, bringing about change, good luck and growth.

New Moon Colours
Green, white, orange and red

New Moon Herbs, Oil and Incense Ingredients
Sandalwood, frankincense, copal, myrrh, rose, saffron, sweet grass, heather, patchouli, cinnamon, lavender, verbena, witch

hazel, jasmine, cardamom, cypress, ginger, nutmeg, orange, chamomile and lemon

New Moon Crystals
Garnet, petalite, sapphire, quartz, labradorite, carnelian, charoite, peridot and phenakite.

New Moon Oil Recipe
4 drops patchouli essential oil
3 drops cedar wood essential oil
4 drops sweet orange essential oil
Add to a base oil such as sweet almond or grape seed (about 15mls of carrier oil should be about right).

New Moon Incense Recipe
2 parts copal resin
2 parts sandalwood
1 part dried rose petals
A few drops of myrrh essential oil

New Moon Meditation
Relax and make yourself comfortable. Close your eyes and focus on your breathing, deep breaths in… and out…Visualise the real world disappearing.

As your world dissipates you find yourself on a high cliff, behind you is a huge eyrie, the nest of an eagle. There is a light breeze, clear blue sky above you and the sun is shining.

You turn to face the eagle and connect mentally with its subconscious… Ask it to show you the pathways and opportunities available to you.

The eagle stands and stretches its huge wings, you realise it is an invitation for you to fly with him. Take some time and gradually shape shift into an eagle. Start with your feet, by morphing them into claws… then stretch your arms out and feel the feathers forming… your fingers

changing... then your head slowly changing to form a beak... gradually you start to feel comfortable in your eagle shape.

A light breeze ruffles your feathers and your eagle companion makes ready to fly. You both perch on the edge of the cliff. The eagle suddenly takes flight... soaring across the sky... you take a deep breath... then leap...

Feel the air beneath you, feel it whisk around your feathers, glide on the current...

Follow the eagle as it soars across the skies...

As you fly take a moment to look down, take in the landscape and the scenery as it rushes past. What you see while flying will give you insight into your options and pathways that are available to you.

Gradually the eagle leads you back to his eyrie.

You land safely on the cliff, exhilarated and full of ideas and plans.

At this point the eagle may give you a message...

When you are ready, slowly change yourself back from an eagle form to your own shape.

Then gradually come back to this reality, stamp your feet and wriggle your fingers.

New Moon Ritual

You will need:
A small plain white candle dressed with sage oil (or dressed with almond/olive oil and rolled in crushed sage leaves)
A goal you wish to achieve, it doesn't have to be grand

Cast the circle by saying:
Maiden cast this circle white
Free from shadow, pure and light
Mother cast this circle red
Cast any negativity from our head
Crone cast this circle black
Grant us the knowledge that we lack

This circle is now cast unbroken.

Call the quarters by saying:
I call to the East and the Element of Air, you who are mist and cloud, you who are fresh breeze and wild hurricane, Spirit of the Hawk, Spirit of the Sylph, hear me, bring into these rites purification and clarity, sweep through and remove stagnation. Blessings and welcome!

I call to the South and the Element of Fire, you who are the crackle of bonfires, you who are the golden Sun and glowing lava, Spirit of the Phoenix, Spirit of the Flame Dancers, hear me, bring into these rites your spirit of creativity and passion. Blessings and welcome!

I call to the West and the Element of Water, you who are the Undines of the rivers, and the sirens of the crashing ocean waves, you who are the Naiads of the Grottos, come to me. Spirit of the Shark, hear me, bring into these rites your deepest intuition and truest emotions, teach me to be flexible, to adapt and flow, like your waters. Blessings and welcome!

I call to the North and the Element of Earth, you who are bone and crystal, you who are tree and root and branch, Spirit of the Wolf, Spirit of the Gnome, I call upon you. Bring into these rites your spirit of prosperity, of stability and manifestation. Blessings and welcome!

Invocation to Deity. Say:
I call upon Vesta, Goddess of the home and the sacred hearth flame, join this rite today and bring with you inspiration and passion. Blessings and welcome!

It is the New Moon, everything is still, but there is a feeling in the air, a sense of something exciting, a building of energy and growth, new potential, new ideas and opportunities. The energy of the New Moon will guide you towards your goals; all you need do is put the ideas forward and into motion. The possibilities are out there and they are endless.

Look inward and find the beginnings of ideas, be prepared to set them in motion.

Now take your white candle and while you light it, repeat quietly to yourself what it is you want to achieve. It doesn't have to be a long-term plan; it can be something quite simple and basic.

Once your candle is burning brightly sit quietly and watch the flame. See how it fires and dances around, so much life, and so much potential. Ask out loud for Vesta to bring you ideas and new opportunities. Spend some time in quiet meditation now and let the ideas come to you...

If possible, allow the candle to burn out (safely).

Thank the quarters by saying:
Guardians to the Element of Earth, I thank you for your presence in this rite, I bid you blessings and farewell.

Guardians to the Element of Water, I thank you for your presence in this rite, I bid you blessings and farewell.

Guardians to the Element of Fire, I thank you for your presence in this rite, I bid you blessings and farewell.

Guardians to the Element of Air, I thank you for your presence in this rite, I bid you blessings and farewell.

Thank Deity by saying:
Vesta, Goddess of the home and sacred hearth flame, I thank you for your presence in this rite, may your flame of inspiration stay with me. Blessings and farewell.

Uncast the circle, walking widdershins, and say:
This circle is open but never broken.

New Moon Spells

I like to write a cheque to myself on the New Moon. I make it out to myself and write 'paid in full' in the amount box, then sign it from 'the law of abundance'. I fold the cheque into three and add three drops of peppermint essential oil on top after laying it in the bottom of a dish I keep on my altar, and then I sprinkle over it dried mint and lay three sticks of cinnamon on top. This works really well to keep enough money coming in.

At the very first sign of the Moon, just the slightest glimpse of her, stand outside and look up. Turn around deosil (sunwise or clockwise) three times and make a wish on the New Moon.

New Moon New Job Spell

If you have decided you need a new job, work this spell on the first night of the New Moon.

What you need:
Two brown candles (to represent your job)
One green candle (for prosperity)
One other coloured candle of your choice (this represents you)
Cinnamon oil
A talisman (this can be a pendant, a pebble, a shell, whatever you wish to use)

Put one of the brown candles in the centre of your altar with the green one to the right of it and your personal candle to the left of it. Put a dab of cinnamon oil on each of the candles.

Light the personal candle and visualise yourself working in the job you would love to do. Next light the green candle and visualise you earning enough money for your needs. Light the brown candle and visualise the company you would like to work for.

Leave the candles to burn out completely and send up a thank you to the Goddess/God/the Divine.

On the next six evenings light the second brown candle and let it burn for six minutes each time and visualise your goal.

When the six nights are up, if you still have some of the brown candle left, bury the remnants in the earth.

Lucky Charm

One of the easiest charms to use for luck is a hag stone (stone with a hole in it). These are found on many beaches and river beds. Leave the stone out on the night of a Waxing Moon, then thread a piece of green ribbon or cord through the hole and wear it as a pendant or hang it from your handbag, your altar or in your car to bring you good luck.

Saving Money Spell

We could all probably do with a bit of extra cash now and then in a savings account for emergencies. Money spells will always work better if we have a real need for the money to cover our basic living costs or specific essential needs rather than just wanting loads of cash to go on a frivolous spending spree!

What you need:
Three gold or silver coins
A green envelope or piece of green paper
Gold or silver thread
Moon water (or rain water works well too)

Hold the coins in your hand and visualise yourself with the money that you need to live on, or purchasing an essential item that you need or have to replace.

When you are ready, put the coins in the envelope or wrap them in the piece of paper and then tie the silver or gold thread around it seven times, visualising your goal as you do so.

Send up your wish and thanks in advance to the Divine and then knot the thread three times. Next, you will need to bury the coin package in the earth, somewhere in your garden (or in a pot on your windowsill) where it will catch the moonlight. Sprinkle the earth where you have buried it with the water.

Waxing Moon

The Waxing Crescent Moon occurs 3½ to 7 days after the New Moon. She rises in the mid-morning and sets in the evening. The Moon's light is quickening. As the Moon has dropped back until she is about ⅛th of the way behind the Sun, we see her lumination as a crescent shape.

You will see the first quarter Moon from 7 to 10½ days after the New Moon. She will rise around noon and set around midnight.

As the Moon is at a right angle to the Sun the difference between high and low tide is minimized. Because light and dark are in balance, the Moon will appear to be a Half Moon, but the area of light will continue to grow each day.

The Waxing Gibbous Moon occurs between 10½ and 14 days after the New Moon. She rises sometime in the mid-afternoon and sets in the early dark hours of the morning.

As the Moon has fallen back around ⅜ of the way behind the Sun, one side of the Moon is seen fully and the light on the other side bulges out, but does not yet fill all of the Moon's face.

Now your projects can get into their stride. Be aware, however, that overstrains are more likely at this time and that the body takes things in and absorbs them more readily with a Waxing Moon.

It is also a good time to build yourself up if you have been unwell or otherwise off-colour. Absorbing, boosting your energy and taking up supplies are crucial now. Go on an active holiday, get in touch with friends, plan a party, arrange meetings and increase communication.

As Full Moon approaches, notice what isn't working and shed it in order to focus your energies more effectively. Remind yourself to slow down a little and conserve your strength. This is a time of regeneration and to gather information and resources.

Waxing Moon Colours

White, pastel colours, red and silver.

Waxing Moon Herbs, Oils and Incense Ingredients

Coriander, geranium, juniper, marjoram, nutmeg, St. John's wort, tansy, thyme, caraway, mace, rosemary, rue, spearmint, bay, carnation, mugwort, pennyroyal, saffron, eucalyptus, cedar, hyacinth, ginger, pine, sandalwood, cinnamon and sweet pea.

Waxing Moon Crystals

Carnelian, citrine, aragonite, green aventurine, malachite, ruby and banded agate.

Waxing Moon Oil Recipe

6 drops lavender essential oil
3 drops basil essential oil
2 drops pine essential oil
1 drop nutmeg essential oil
Add to a base oil such as sweet almond or grape seed (about 15mls of carrier oil should be about right).

Waxing Moon Incense Recipe

2 parts juniper
2 parts cedar
1 part pine
1 part eucalyptus

Waxing Moon Meditation

Make yourself comfortable, close your eyes and focus on your breathing... deep breaths in and out... Visualise the real world disappearing.

As your world dissipates you find yourself at the foot of a hill, the grass is green beneath your feet and you can feel a gentle breeze on your face.

The lush grass is scattered with white daisies and you can smell their fresh scent in the air.

A small narrow track leads up the side of the hill in front of you, twisting and turning, spiralling its way up to the top, so you decide to follow it.

As you walk, following the path round and up with each step, release any stresses and worries that you are carrying with you...

Look out across the scenery, what do you see? What sounds can you hear?

Look out for any wildlife along the way.

Take deep breaths of cleansing, refreshing air as you walk. Walk on, continuing to ascend the path, heading always upwards.

When you reach the top of the hill you lay down on the grass, lying on your back and looking up at the sky. Watch the white, wispy clouds as they float past in the bright blue sky. What shapes do you see?

In the distance you see a darker cloud and realise that in the opposite valley there is a light rain shower, but the sun is still shining on your hilltop. After a short while a beautiful rainbow appears.

As you lie on the hilltop, allow yourself to draw renewing, invigorating energy from the rainbow, it is a gift from Mother Nature and she is happy to share it. Take as much energy as you need.

When you are ready, stand up and take a long look around at the landscape.

Then start to make your way back down the hillside, slowly following the pathway as it spirals down until you reach the foot of the hill.

Give thanks to Mother Nature and come back to this reality. Stamp your feet and wriggle your fingers.

Waxing Moon Ritual

You will need:
Two light blue candles, one white
Rosemary

Piece of paper
Quartz tumble stone

Cast the circle, saying:

> *Maiden cast this circle white*
> *Free from shadow, pure and light*
> *Mother cast this circle red*
> *Cast any negativity from our head*
> *Crone cast this circle black*
> *Grant us the knowledge that we lack*
> *This circle is now cast unbroken.*

Call the quarters, saying:

> *I call to the East and the Element of Air, you who are mist and cloud, you who are fresh breeze and wild hurricane, Spirit of the Hawk, Spirit of the Sylph, hear me, bring into these rites purification and clarity, sweep through and remove stagnation. Blessings and welcome!*
>
> *I call to the South and the Element of Fire, you who are the crackle of bonfires, you who are the golden Sun and glowing lava, Spirit of the Phoenix, Spirit of the Flame Dancers, hear me, bring into these rites your spirit of creativity and passion. Blessings and welcome!*
>
> *I call to the West and the Element of Water, you who are the Undines of the rivers, and the Sirens of the crashing ocean waves, you who are the Naiads of the Grottos, come to me. Spirit of the Shark, hear me, bring into these rites your deepest intuition and truest emotions, teach me to be flexible, to adapt and flow, like your waters. Blessings and welcome!*
>
> *I call to the North and the Element of Earth, you who are bone and crystal, you who are tree and root and branch, Spirit of the Wolf, Spirit of the Gnome, I call upon you. Bring into these rites*

your spirit of prosperity, of stability and manifestation. Blessings and welcome!

Invocation to Deity:

I call upon the Goddess Athene, join this rite today and wave your wisdom and philosophy into this rite. Blessings and welcome!

It is the time of the Waxing Moon, a period of new beginnings, improving your health, attracting good luck, finding friendships, new jobs and making plans for the future.

Place the candles on your altar in front of you in a semi-circle shape, the white candle between the two blue ones. Place the rosemary by the white candle. Write the name of the person who needs healing or good health on the piece of paper and lay that in the middle of the semi-circle of candles. Place the crystal on top of the paper.

Light the candles then visualise the person in question in good health, happy and fit. When you are ready, send the energy from your visualisation into the crystal and through to the piece of paper beneath it.

The crystal can now be given to the person in question to carry with them for continued good health. The candle stubs can be buried in the earth along with the piece of paper.

Thank the quarters, saying:

Guardians to the Element of Earth, I thank you for your presence in this rite, I bid you blessings and farewell.
Guardians to the Element of Water, I thank you for your presence in this rite, I bid you blessings and farewell.
Guardians to the Element of Fire, I thank you for your presence in this rite, I bid you blessings and farewell.
Guardians to the Element of Air, I thank you for your presence in this rite, I bid you blessings and farewell.

Thank Deity:

Athene, Goddess of weaving, I thank you for your presence in this rite, may your wisdom and philosophy stay with me. Blessings and farewell.

Uncast the circle, walking widdershins (anti-sunwise) and say:

This circle is open but never broken.

Waxing Moon Lemon Spell
The lemon is ruled by the power of the Moon and works very well in this spell.

Use an unripe lemon if possible, then using dress-making pins (the ones with the coloured heads work best). Stick the pins into the lemon. As you put each pin into the rind state out loud your intent, so you could put a pin in and ask for prosperity, the next one might be for happiness, the next for good health etc... you get the idea. When you are done, place the lemon on your altar, or you could hang it above your front door to bring positive energy into the house.

Waxing Moon Health Spell
Use eucalyptus on the Waxing Moon to bring good health and healing; use the essential oil on a candle, or burn the leaves in incense, alternatively, add them to a medicine pouch.

Waxing Moon Spell For Confidence
We all need a bit of a confidence boost every so often so give this little spell a try.

What you need:
A malachite crystal
A white candle

A green candle

If you would like to, you can dress your altar with white flowers and add some sprigs of green parsley.

Set the green and white candle on your altar and sit in front of them, light them both.

Take the malachite crystal in your hand and ask out loud for help from the Divine for courage, confidence and communication skills. Visualise yourself as being full of confidence. Touch the crystal to your mouth for the blessings of communication, to your ears for the power of listening and understanding, and then to your throat for the blessings of confidence.

Focus your thoughts on the candle flames until they burn out, keeping hold of the crystal as you do so. You can then carry the crystal with you in a pocket, purse or bag.

Waxing Moon Resolution Spell

Sometimes, when we have resolved to do something or stick to a regime, our resolution wavers. This spell will help strengthen it.

You will need:
A purple candle
White thread

Start by winding the cotton three times deosil (clockwise) around the candle, about a third of the way down. As you do so, focus on your breathing, taking deep breaths in and out. On the third wrap of the cotton take a deep breath in and hold it for a count of six. Visualise yourself being surrounded in purple light to give you strength.

When you are ready, light the candle and focus on the flame. As you do so, ask out loud for strength in your resolve and help with keeping your focus on the task. End with the words '*and harm to none, so mote it be*'.

Crescent Moon Cookies

These are lovely to make to eat during (or after... or both) your Moon ritual.

You will need:
1 ½ cups (190g) all purpose (plain) flour
1 ½ teaspoons baking soda
1 ½ teaspoons baking powder
1 cup (225g) butter (softened)
2 ½ cups (375g) sugar
1 egg
1 teaspoon vanilla extract

Preheat the oven to 350 degrees.

Cream the butter and sugar together until the mixture is light and creamy.

Add the egg, butter and sugar and mix them together well.

In a separate bowl mix together the flour, baking powder and baking soda.

Then gradually add the dry ingredient mix to the wet ingredients, mix until it becomes dough.

Flour your hands and roll the dough into small ball shapes (about the size of a golf ball). Flatten each ball shape down and make it into a crescent shape. You can also just roll the dough out and use crescent shape cookie cutters (you will need to flour the cutter before each use so it doesn't stick).

Bake the biscuits on an ungreased baking tray for about ten minutes.

Crescent Moon Magic

This is magic worked as the Moon rises at mid-morning and sets after sunset. It is good for animals, business, change, emotions, matriarchal strength. This phase of the Moon represents zest of life with the aid of stability. It helps bring forth courage and optimism.

Gibbous Moon Magic

The Gibbous Moon is almost full, but not completely full. The magic of this phase is good for patience, purity and protection. It creates atmosphere for meditation and centring. It can symbolise innocence.

Full Moon

About 15 days after the after the New Moon, the Full Moon first appears. At this point the Moon is on the opposite side of the Earth from the Sun, so she rises around sunset and sets around dawn.

The Sun shines fully on her face and tides are at their extremes again. Some may sense the pull of the Sun from one direction, and the Moon from the opposite, and their energy will feel a bit scattered.

Hold a party or an event, but be aware that the energy level is likely to be high and anything troublesome is likely to surface. Cook and stock up the freezer. Pay special attention to your creative ventures and your dreams.

This is a good time to try out forms of divinations such as scrying or tarot. Reflect about your goals, feelings and matters that have to do with relationship and family. It is also good for transformations, psychic abilities, strength, love, power and fertility.

The Full Moon is also an excellent time to cleanse, purify and charge your crystals. Lay them out so that the moonlight can hit them; if you can do so safely, leave them outside. If not, find a windowsill that catches the moonlight. Don't just stop at crystals though, your magical tools will also benefit from soaking up the power of the moonlight.

As the Full Moon just passes, the time arrives to put the finishing touches on what you have been doing and to get ready for the quieter time to come. Enjoy beauty and art, listen to music. If you have argued with someone but do not feel the issues are really vital, make up now.

If you live near the sea the Full Moon is a wonderful time to visit the shoreline and (if safe and legal to do so) build a small fire. Collect small pieces of driftwood to build your fire and, as you lay each piece onto the fire, add a wish. Once the fire is burning nicely, cast offerings into the flames as gifts to the Moon Goddess, such as herbs, flowers and leaves. Sit and watch as the fire burns. If you don't live near the sea you could turn this into a visualisation for a Full Moon meditation.

Full Moon Colours
Blue, white, yellow and orange

Full Moon Herbs, Oils and Incense Ingredients
Frankincense, sandalwood, rose, cedar, juniper berry, hyssop, myrtle, orange, rosewood, tangerine, tea tree, yarrow and sage.

Full Moon Crystals
Moonstone, selenite, quartz, black tourmaline, obsidian, amber, rose quartz and opal.

Full Moon Oil Recipe
6 drops gardenia essential oil
4 drops lotus essential oil
2 drops jasmine essential oil
Add to a base oil such as sweet almond or grape seed (about 15mls of carrier oil should be about right).

Full Moon Balm (for pulse points)
6 drops sandalwood essential oil
3 drops lemon essential oil
2 drops palma rose essential oil
¼ cup grated beeswax
¼ cup vegetable oil
Melt oil and wax together, cool slightly then stir in essential oils. Store in an airtight pot.

Full Moon Incense (loose mix to burn on charcoal disc)

2 parts sandalwood
2 parts frankincense resin
¼ part dried rose petals
½ part orris root
6 drops sandalwood oil

Moon Magic Bath Salts

1 cup sea salt
8 drops sandalwood essential oil
8 drops lotus essential oil
Mix together and store in an airtight container, sprinkle a couple of tablespoons of the mixture in you bath.

Full Moon Meditation

Relax and make yourself comfortable, close your eyes and focus on your breathing, deep breaths in and out... Visualise the real word disappearing.

As your world dissipates you find yourself on the edge of a forest. It is night-time and the sky is a deep, dark blue, but it is scattered with thousands of sparkling stars and the Moon is full and bright, bright enough to light your way.

You enter the forest between two yew trees, the air is cool and you can smell the earthy scent of the forest floor. There appears to be a small pathway between the trees, which you start to follow. The leaves crackle under foot and you can hear the sounds of birds and wildlife above and all around you.

You follow the path until it leads to a clearing. As you leave the trees you step into dappled sunlight... in the centre of the clearing is a deep pool of water, the surface of which is perfectly still.

You walk right up to the edge of the pool and sit down beside it.

As you gaze into the water you realise the Full Moon above you is reflected onto the surface of the dark water.

You put your hand down and trail your fingers through the water which sends ripples across the surface.

You centre your thoughts and think of a question or situation you need an answer or clarity to...

Look to the surface of the water for signs and symbols... what do you see?

Above you a hoot sounds out across the woods and, with a flapping of wings, a huge owl takes flight from a tree above you and flies across the clearing.

When you have finished your scrying stand up and make your way back to the pathway and head to the edge of the forest.

Slowly bring yourself back to this reality, stamp your feet and wriggle your fingers.

Full Moon Ritual

You will need:
A cauldron (or dish with a dark inside) half filled with water
A small silver coin

Cast the circle, saying:

> *Maiden cast this circle white*
> *Free from shadow, pure and light*
> *Mother cast this circle red*
> *Cast any negativity from our head*
> *Crone cast this circle black*
> *Grant us the knowledge that we lack*
> *This circle is now cast unbroken.*

Call the quarters, saying:

> *I call to the East and the Element of Air, you who are mist and cloud, you who are fresh breeze and wild hurricane, Spirit of the Hawk, Spirit of the Sylph, hear me, bring into these rites purification and*

clarity, sweep through and remove stagnation. Blessings and welcome!

I call to the South and the Element of Fire, you who are the crackle of bonfires, you who are the golden Sun and glowing lava, Spirit of the Phoenix, Spirit of the Flame Dancers, hear me, bring into these rites your spirit of creativity and passion. Blessings and welcome!

I call to the West and the Element of Water, you who are the Undines of the rivers, and the Sirens of the crashing ocean waves, you who are the Naiads of the Grottos, come to me. Spirit of the Shark, hear me, bring into these rites your deepest intuition and truest emotions, teach me to be flexible, to adapt and flow, like your waters. Blessings and welcome!

I call to the North and the Element of Earth, you who are bone and crystal, you who are tree and root and branch, Spirit of the Wolf, Spirit of the Gnome, I call upon you. Bring into these rites your spirit of prosperity, of stability and manifestation. Blessings and welcome!

Invocation to Deity:

I call upon Yemaya, Goddess of the seas, join this rite today and bring with you feminine energy and healing. Blessings and welcome!

The Full Moon is a powerful time; she carries with her magic to aid in immediate need, power boosts, courage, psychic protection and healing. This Moon phase can also bring urgently needed money, commitment, justice and ambition.

Sit quietly in front of your cauldron of water and drop a silver coin into the water, if you can position the cauldron so that the moonlight reflects into it even better. You can gather the Moon's energy by skimming your hand just across the top of the water.

Say a chant to the Goddess and the Full Moon asking for

enough money to cover your needs. Visualise the goal.

Leave the water and the coin in the cauldron until the following day when you can tip the water onto the earth.

Thank the quarters, saying:

Guardians to the Element of Earth, I thank you for your presence in this rite, I bid you blessings and farewell.
Guardians to the Element of Water, I thank you for your presence in this rite, I bid you blessings and farewell.
Guardians to the Element of Fire, I thank you for your presence in this rite, I bid you blessings and farewell.
Guardians to the Element of Air, I thank you for your presence in this rite, I bid you blessings and farewell.

Thank Deity:

Goddess Yemaya, I thank you for your presence in this rite, may your energy and healing stay with me. Blessings and farewell.

Uncast the circle, walking widdershins, saying:

This circle is open but never broken.

Making Moon Water

Moon water is really simple to make and can be used for all sorts of spell work, rituals and anointing. It is useful to have in stock when you need to use the power of the Moon phase at a different time.

Using a dish, bowl or bottle, fill it with spring water and leave it outside (if it can be safely done) or on a windowsill so that it can soak up the power of the Full Moon. You can also do the same process on the New, Waxing, Waning or Dark Moon phases too. Once the water has absorbed the power of the Moon, you can keep it in an airtight bottle for future use.

You can also add a pinch of sea salt to the water to give it extra cleansing and purifying oomph.

Camellia Money Spell

I have a beautiful camellia bush in my garden that is covered with pink blossoms. I pick up the flowers once they have dropped on the ground in spring and place them on my altar, as they stay in perfect condition for several days afterwards.

The camellia brings riches and luxury, and so is used in spells of this kind.

Place the blossoms in vessels of water on your altar during money and prosperity rituals, or use them in spells.

The lovely Moon-ruled blooms of the Camellia are ideal for money spells. Just before Full Moon, place a bowl of them on your altar and drop three silver coins in between the blooms, naming one for money to spend, one for a loved one to spend it on and the third for the wisdom to spend it wisely. When your rite is over, take the three coins and keep them in a piece of cotton. Press one of the flowers between two sheets of tissue paper and keep that with the coins as your fortune begins to grow.

When casting Full Moon spells it is best to go outside during the night of a Full Moon. Go to a location where you will not be disturbed. Face the direction of the Moon.

Full Moon Wish Spell

Take a couple of pennies and go outside where you can clearly see the Full Moon. Hold the pennies in your hand and ask out loud that your wish be granted. Visualise what your goal is... and state it out loud. Throw the pennies up into the air towards the Moon. Then say out loud that you offer the pennies to the Moon and give thanks.

Lemon Balm for Love

Lemon balm grows like a wild thing in my garden, so much so that I have had to contain it in pots! It is a plant that is ruled by the Moon.

For this spell soak a few lemon balm leaves in apple juice (also a fruit of love), leave the mixture in a place where it can capture the light of the Full Moon then share the drink with your partner using the same cup, this should ensure a strong and true love.

Arianrhod's Silver Wheel Divination

This is a fun project to make and do. Be creative and go with your instincts on what materials to use.

Take a piece of square cloth, you will need to draw a circle in the centre of it (or sew, embroider – whatever skills you have!) Then mark the circle into quarters. Within the centre of each circle draw (or sew) a phase of the Moon – a black circle for the Dark Moon, a crescent for the Waxing Moon, a white circle for the Full Moon and a crescent for the Waning Moon. (Drawing around a coin might help keep the circles an even shape).

Next you will need 13 stones. You can either use tumble stone crystals that you might already have, or purchase them specifically for this or collect natural pebbles from the beach or riverbed.

You will need to identify each stone, so coloured tumble stone crystals are easier, but you could mark natural pebbles as well, preferably three red, three green, three blue, three brown and one black. A bag is useful to keep them all in.

You can go with your own meanings and correspondences for each stone or each colour group but a good guideline is:

- Red stones represent energy, career and the future.
- Blue stones represent mental energy, communication, thoughts, study and the present.
- Green stones represent healing, love, family and the past.

- Brown stones represent money, physical body, practical things and the very distant past.
- The black stone is the unknown, surprises and mysteries.

When you have all your items ready, ground and centre yourself, then form a question in your mind. Draw a stone from the bag without looking at it, hold your hand above the cloth and let the stone fall. Repeat this process three times. If the stone falls outside the circle on the cloth then it is disregarded.

The first stone you cast surrounds your situation, the second stone represents current conditions and the third stone is the outcome. If you aren't clear on the reading you can draw a fourth stone for clarification.

Depending on which quarter of the circle the stone drops in will bear relation to the colour of the stone, and therefore, the answer to your question. Use the meanings of the phases of the Moon to relate to the stone, so the Waxing Moon segment would mean revealing or growth.

Go with your intuition!

Disseminating Moon Magic

This is when the Moon is just past being full, and appears slightly flat on one side. This phase is good for addictions, decisions, divorce, emotions, stress, and protection. It builds knowledge, sharing, calming, vocal expression and communication. The Disseminating Moon also aids meditation and enhances inner attunement.

Waning Moon

The Waning Gibbous Moon or Disseminating Moon appears 3½ days to 7 days after the Full Moon. The Moon will rise during the evening and set sometime mid-morning. Again we see the bulge on one side of the Moon but it is now decreasing each day. Darkness is slowly moving in. Waning is underway.

The Waning Last Quarter Moon appears between 7 and 10½ days after the Full Moon. She rises near midnight and sets near noon. Because of the return to a right angle between the Sun and Moon the variation between tides is low again. There is once again a balance between light and dark, but the dark will soon overcome the light.

The Waning Crescent or Balsamic Moon occurs between 10½ days after the Full Moon up until the New Moon. The Moon rises in the dark hours of the morning and sets in the afternoon. Again we see the Moon as a beautiful crescent, but it is rapidly diminishing into darkness.

You do not have to be concerned so much about overdoing things now because the lunar rhythm will act as something of a brake. Now is a good time to throw away your rubbish, take old clothes to charity shops. Consider how well things are working out and analyse information. Follow your needs and reactions.

You may feel more like meditating and being alone. Clear spaces of all descriptions and make endings, let go of unwanted energies, release, banish and reverse. Some people favour scrying and meditation with the Dark Moon because it is a more inward time. The insights you glean now will have a deeper more insightful quality, whereas as Full Moon they may be more obviously creative.

To connect with the Waxing Moon energies and the energy of the Crone, place an amethyst in a bowl of water, light a purple candle and scry.

Use a hag stone (holey stone) or a piece of elder or yew wood. Hold this during meditation to connect with crone energies and the energy of the Waning Moon.

Make a crone hearth in your fireplace or on your mantelpiece. Decorate it with symbols that represent her to you, or you could just use a cauldron (or big casserole dish) and fill it with a large dark coloured candle and pebbles.

Waning Moon Colours
Blue, purple and pink.

Waning Moon herbs, Oils and Incense Ingredients
Anise, bay, eucalyptus, cypress, frankincense, hyssop, jasmine, lime, marjoram, myrtle, orange, sandalwood, tangerine, tea tree, sage, lavender and yarrow.

Waning Moon Crystals
Smokey quartz, rhodochrosite, rose quartz, rhodonite, ruby in fuchsite, pink kunzite and danburite.

Waning Moon Bath Salts
1 cup sea salt
3 drops geranium essential oil
3 drops pine essential oil
6 drops magnolia essential oil

Waning Moon Oil Recipe
4 drops cypress essential oil
3 drops clove essential oil
3 drops cedar wood essential oil
Add to a base oil such as sweet almond or grape seed (about 15mls of carrier oil should be about right).

Waning Moon Incense Recipe

3 parts frankincense resin

2 parts myrrh

1 part sandalwood

A few drops of sandalwood essential oil

Make a Crone Circlet

This is lovely to wear during a Waning Moon ritual. Take a base of wire and add leaves, flowers and twigs. Use dark coloured ribbon, such as dark purples, blues and black, to decorate it. As you make the circlet add in the intent of your dreams and wishes that you wish to fulfil.

Waning Moon Meditation

Relax and make yourself comfortable, close your eyes and focus on your breathing, deep breaths in... and out... Visualise the real world disappearing.

As your world dissipates you find yourself on a beach. The waves are crashing onto the shore in front of you and you can smell the salt in the air. As you turn around there is a rocky landscape behind you. As you look you can see a gap between the rocks so you go to investigate. You squeeze through the gap and find yourself in a passageway of rocks.

As you follow the corridor of rock it suddenly opens out into a small paradise scene. You are surrounded by palm trees and in front of you is a huge waterfall. The sound of the water is very loud but beautiful. You can feel the power of it in your chest.

Make your way to the edge of the waterfall... as you get closer you can just make out a cave behind the curtain of water.

You suddenly feel the urge to step into the cascading water. You step carefully and end up standing directly below the waterfall. It is cool and refreshing.

As you allow the water to fall over you, let go of old habits, negative energies and anything that does not serve your higher good. Let the water wash it all away.

When you are finished you feel refreshed and renewed.

Step back out of the cascading water and sit down beside it. Now take some time to think about all the positive things in your life, fill your mind with happy thoughts and new goals.

Then stand up and make your way back to the passageway through the rocks and back out to the shore.

Take a moment to watch the waves and when you are ready come back to this reality, stamp your feet and wriggle your toes.

Waning Moon Ritual

You will need:
Large leaf herbs that you associate with the Moon (see list below).
A dark candle

Soak a pinch of the herbs in a bowl of salt water overnight if possible. Then remove them from the water and leave them to dry.

Cast the circle, saying:

Maiden cast this circle white
Free from shadow, pure and light
Mother cast this circle red
Cast any negativity from our head
Crone cast this circle black
Grant us the knowledge that we lack
This circle is now cast unbroken.

Call the quarters, saying:

I call to the East and the Element of Air, you who are mist and cloud, you who are fresh breeze and wild hurricane, Spirit of the Hawk, Spirit of the Sylph, hear me, bring into these rites purifi-

cation and clarity, sweep through and remove stagnation. Blessings and welcome!

I call to the South and the Element of Fire, you who are the crackle of bonfires, you who are the golden Sun and glowing lava, Spirit of the Phoenix, Spirit of the Flame Dancers, hear me, bring into these rites your spirit of creativity and passion. Blessings and welcome!

I call to the West and the Element of Water, you who are the Undines of the rivers, and the Sirens of the crashing ocean waves, you who are the Naiads of the Grottos, come to me. Spirit of the Shark, hear me, bring to these rites your deepest intuition and truest emotions, teach me to be flexible, to adapt and flow, like your waters. Blessings and welcome!

I call to the North and the Element of Earth, you who are bone and crystal, you who are tree and root and branch, Spirit of the Wolf, Spirit of the Gnome, I call upon you. Bring to these rites your spirit of prosperity, of stability and manifestation. Blessings and welcome!

Invocation to Deity:

I call upon Diana, Goddess of the witches and the hunt, join this rite today and bring with you magic and protection. Blessings and welcome!

The Waning Moon phase is good for removing things, getting rid of obstacles, relieving illness and pain, banishing negative thoughts, releasing pain, guilt anger, anxiety and bad habits. It's time to let go of all that does not serve your higher good!

Place your dark candle in a suitable holder, put it on your altar and light it (don't light any other candles on your altar).

Take the dried, salted herb leaves and slowly burn each one in the flame of the candle (you might want to drop them into a cauldron or flame-proof dish as you do this, as the salt will make the flame spit). As each leaf burns say out loud what it is you wish to be rid of, burn the bad habits, bad cycles, unwanted energies and say goodbye to that which no longer serves you for the greater good.

When you have burnt all the herbs, sit quietly in front of the candle and clear out the negative thoughts from your mind and replace them with positive ones. Fill the void that you have just made with happy images and new plans.

If possible, allow the candle to burn out (safely).

Thank the quarters, saying:

Guardians to the Element of Earth, I thank you for your presence in this rite, I bid you blessings and farewell.
Guardians to the Element of Water, I thank you for your presence in this rite, I bid you blessings and farewell.
Guardians to the Element of Fire, I thank you for your presence in this rite, I bid you blessings and farewell.
Guardians to the Element of Air, I thank you for your presence in this rite, I bid you blessings and farewell.

Thank Deity, saying:

Diana, goddess of the witches and the hunt, I thank you for your presence in this rite, may your magic and protection stay with me. Blessings and farewell.

Uncast the circle, walking widdershins. Say:

This circle is open but never broken.

Waning Moon Releasing Worry and Stress Spell

What you need:
White candle
Black candle

Pink candle

Light a white candle to symbolise peace. While watching the flame, meditate on the question, what does peace mean to you?

Next light a black candle, this will absorb negative energies. Visualise any worries or stresses that you have being taken from you and into the black candle, which will transform that energy into positive vibes.

Now take a piece of paper and write down something that you wish to release or transform, then light the corner of the paper on the candle flame and drop it into your cauldron (or flame proof dish). Allow it to burn out and, as it does so, let it too take your worries and stresses with it. You can repeat this part as many times as you feel you need to.

When you are ready, snuff out the black candle. Next light a pink candle and focus on filling that void with positive and happy thoughts, wishes and plans.

When you banish negative energy you MUST fill it with positive energy otherwise the negative pattern will be repeated.

When you are finished, snuff out the pink and white candles.

You can repeat this spell over the course of several days until you feel you are done. If there are any candle stubs left bury them in the earth.

Waning Moon Reversing Spell

On occasion, unfortunately we may feel like we have been hit with a curse, a run of bad luck or even perhaps someone sending negative energy our way. This spell will reverse it.

What you need:
A small mirror
A black candle
A small dish of water

You need to set the mirror so that you can sit comfortably in front of it and see the reflection of your face, and also the reflection of the candle. Keep the room dark if possible and light the candle. Visualise any negative energy that has been sent your way or bad luck that has beset you being reflected away from you. As you visualise this happening, slowly move backwards away from the mirror until you are out of focus and the only reflection that remains in the mirror is the candle flame. When you feel all the negative energy has been reflected away, put out the candle with the water. Bury the candle stub in the earth.

Waning Moon Spell to Banish Depression

Depression is quite frankly horrible and sometimes it can be an incredibly difficult frame of mind to get out of. Working this spell on the Waning Moon phase can help.

You will need:
A few black candles
Water (preferably spring water)
A glass jug
A handful of soil made into mud with a little tap water
A glass bowl
Rose petals

Light a black candle and fill the glass jug with water, leaving about an inch free at the top. Stand the jug in front of the candle and focus on the flame, see the flame as the light in the dark tunnel, the light represents your life before the depression cloud came into it. Now put the handful of mud into the jug of water. Watch as the mud makes the water cloudy, visualise that mud as your depression. See the mud and your depression being dissolved in the water, allowing yourself to be released from its hold.

Snuff the candle out but leave it and the jug where they are.

Fill the glass bowl with water and sprinkle the rose petals on the surface. Wash your hands in the water.

The next day, light another black candle and replace the first one. See the water clearing gradually. Keep lighting a new candle each day and visualising the water as your life, being freed from the grip of depression.

When you are ready throw the water away, as far away as you can (outside of course!) and let that water carry any remaining threads of depression away with it.

Dark Moon/Balsamic

This is the time after the Waning Moon has disappeared from view and before the New Moon is visible, when the sky is dark and there is nothing to see. The sky is literally 'completely dark'.

This phase is magically good for addictions, change, divorce, enemies, justice, obstacles, quarrels, removal, separation, stopping stalkers and theft.

It can also be associated with universal love of self and others. The Dark Moon energy draws love to you and removes sorrows and past hurts. Calming, protective and serene, it improves relationships. This is also a good time for divination.

When the last quarter of the Moon has disappeared, write the name of something you wish to decrease on to the side of a black candle, and burn it every night until the New Moon. (Be careful here, you might want to state 'and harm none'). Leave your altar bare of flowers at this time. Burn only dark coloured candles or none at all. Use sombre incense such as myrrh and patchouli. Raise energy with slow drumming or chanting, or keep your rites low key. Call on the wisdom of the crone goddesses. Use this time to eliminate or banish bad habits.

You may feel more like meditating and being alone. Clear spaces of all descriptions and make endings. Some people favour scrying and meditation with the Dark Moon because it is a more inward time. The insights you glean now will have a deeper more insightful quality, whereas at Full Moon they may be more obviously creative.

Dark Moon Colours
Black, dark purple, dark blue.

Dark Moon Crystals
Obsidian, apache tears, rainbow obsidian.

Dark Moon Herbs, Oils and Incense Ingredients

Myrrh, bay, frankincense, jasmine, rose, elder, damiana, angelica, sage, borage, cinnamon, marigold, mugwort, rowan, saffron, star anise, thyme, camphor, dandelion, pomegranate, patchouli and yarrow.

Dark Moon Oil Recipe

7 drops jasmine essential oil
3 drops patchouli essential oil
1 drop sandalwood essential oil
Add these to a base oil such as sweet almond or grape seed (about 15mls of carrier oil should be about right).

Dark Moon Incense Recipe:

1 part dried jasmine flowers
1 part myrrh resin
1 part dried rose petals
½ part dried elder leaves
A few drops of myrrh essential oil

Dark Moon Bath Salts

1 cup sea salt
8 drops magnolia essential oil
3 drops pine essential oil
4 drops geranium essential oil

Dark Moon Meditation

Relax and make yourself comfortable, close your eyes and focus on your breathing, deep breaths in and out... Visualise the real world disappearing.

As your world dissipates around you, find yourself at the entrance to a cave. Outside there is a fire burning with a large cauldron on a stand hanging above it.

You make your way to the fire and begin to take in the delicious aroma wafting from the pot.

Surrounding the fire are blankets and cushions. As you reach the fire you hear the sound of movements from within the cave. Then an old crone appears from the cave mouth carrying a bunch of dried herbs. She looks up and greets you with a nod and invites you to join her, gesturing for you to sit on the cushions surrounding the fire.

As you make yourself comfortable she drops the dried herbs into the cauldron and gives it a stir, creating more of the delicious scent to fill the air. She then sits herself down next to you and stares into the flames of the fire. After a short while she turns to you and asks, 'What are you searching for, child?'

You ponder her question for a moment and then answer her...

She sits quietly for a few moments and then gives you her answer. You reply to her with any other queries you have, she responds with her thoughts.

When you have finished talking she reaches into her pocket, draws her hand back out and hands an item to you. Take it and thank her.

When you are ready stand up and thank the crone.

Make your way back to this reality, stamp your feet and wriggle your fingers. What did the crone gift you with and what meaning does it have for you?

Dark Moon Ritual

You will need:
A green candle
A cauldron or flame proof dish
Paper and pen

Cast the circle, saying:

> *Maiden cast this circle white*
> *Free from shadow, pure and light*
> *Mother cast this circle red*

Cast any negativity from our head
Crone cast this circle black
Grant us the knowledge that we lack
This circle is now cast unbroken.

Calling the quarters, saying:

I call to the East and the Element of Air, you who are mist and cloud, you who are fresh breeze and wild hurricane, Spirit of the Hawk, Spirit of the Sylph, hear me, bring into these rites purification and clarity, sweep through and remove stagnation. Blessings and welcome!

I call to the South and the Element of Fire, you who are the crackle of bonfires, you who are the golden Sun and glowing lava, Spirit of the Phoenix, Spirit of the Flame Dancers, hear me, bring into these rites your spirit of creativity and passion. Blessings and welcome!

I call to the West and the Element of Water, you who are the Undines of the rivers, and the Sirens of the crashing ocean waves, you who are the Naiads of the Grottos, come to me. Spirit of the Shark, hear me, bring into these rites your deepest intuition and truest emotions, teach me to be flexible, to adapt and flow, like your waters. Blessings and welcome!

I call to the North and the Element of Earth, you who are bone and crystal, you who are tree and root and branch, Spirit of the Wolf, Spirit of the Gnome, I call upon you. Bring into these rites your spirit of prosperity, of stability and manifestation. Blessings and welcome!

Invocation to Deity. Say:

I call upon Arianrhod, Dark Moon Goddess and Lady of the Silver wheel, join this rite today and bring with you powers of renewal and rebirth. Blessings and welcome!

Use the power of the Dark Moon to look within, take time to contemplate. You removed all those unwanted energies at the Waning Moon, now it is time to go inwards and see what your real desires are.

Light your green candle.

Take your paper and write your dreams and desires on them, as many as you wish with one goal per piece of paper. Stack them on top of each other and place them in front of you.

If you are using a wand or an athame (ceremonial knife), tap each piece of paper, one at a time. Visualise powerful white light coming from the end and pulsing through the paper (if you aren't using any tools just use your finger tip). Then light each paper from the green candle and drop it into the cauldron or dish. As you do so each time send a blessing to the Divine.

When you are finished, snuff the candle out. After the ritual, take the ashes from the paper and either cast them into flowing water or bury them in the earth.

You might also like to sit for a while and meditate. Ask Arianrhod to show you at least some of your past lives...

Thank the quarters. Say:

Guardians to the Element of Earth, I thank you for your presence in this rite, I bid you blessings and farewell.
Guardians to the Element of Water, I thank you for your presence in this rite, I bid you blessings and farewell.
Guardians to the Element of Fire, I thank you for your presence in this rite, I bid you blessings and farewell.
Guardians to the Element of Air, I thank you for your presence in this rite, I bid you blessings and farewell.

Thank Deity, saying:

Arianrhod, Dark Moon Goddess and Lady of the Silver Wheel, I thank you for your presence in this rite, may your powers of renewal stay with me. Blessings and farewell.

Uncast the circle, walking widdershins. Say:

This circle is open but never broken.

Dark Moon Dream Charm
The beautiful flowers of the jasmine are ruled by the Moon. They work especially well in a medicine pouch or incense blend on the Dark Moon to bring about deep and meaningful dreams.

Dark Moon Spell to Protect Your House
This one is seriously easy and will place your home in a protective shell.

The only item you need for this spell is your own power. Sit quietly in the centre of your home, relax and centre yourself. Get a visualisation of your house into your mind. Take in all the details then, drawing on energy from Mother Earth, see a ring of powerful white protective light come up from the Earth around the boundaries of your property. Watch as it grows upwards and forms a protective bubble around your home.

The protective shield is now in place around your house. Every so often when you have a moment just sit and strengthen the shield with your mind and the power of Mother Earth energy.

Dark Moon Spell to Move Forward
Life lessons can occasionally leave us floundering and wondering how to pick up the pieces and move on with life. This spell should help.

What you need:
A photograph of the person involved (such as your ex) or an image of the situation that caused your life to fall apart
A cauldron or fire-proof dish

A sprig of leaves or herbs of your choice

A small pouch or bag (I use the little wedding favour bags you can pick up easily from craft stores or a small pouch made from felt).

Set light to the corner of the photograph and drop it into the cauldron to burn. Watch the flame and visualise all the pain, hurt and anguish you have experienced being released from you. Keep visualising the smoke from the flame taking those negative energies away. When you are ready, take the sprig of herbs/leaves and hold them in your hands. Send whatever negative energies you have remaining into those herbs, then bring your hands up to your forehead and visualise happy and joyful images replacing the hurtful and negative ones.

End by putting the herbs and ashes of the photograph into the pouch or bag. Take it away from your house and bury it. (I also find that throwing it in the dustbin the day the bins are emptied works too, as the dustbin truck takes care of removing it for me!)

When you dispose of the pouch take a minute or two to remember the good times you had before trouble set in.

Blue Moon, Red Moon and Eclipses

Blue Moon

Every so often we get a second Full Moon in a month and sometimes we actually get four Full Moons in a single season. Such Full Moons are called Blue Moons or sometimes 'Goal Moons'. Sadly the Moon doesn't actually change colour, it looks just the same as the usual Full Moon.

The term 'Blue Moon' seems to only be a few hundred years old. References in history to a Blue Moon were improbable events or things that would not normally happen. This evolved to mean a rare occurrence or happening, and has led to the saying 'once in a blue moon'.

There is a belief that the Blue Moon holds the knowledge of the Crone and, therefore, all the wisdom of the Triple Goddesses combined. It is also said that the Blue Moon brings a time of heightened communication and connection with the Divine and the spirit world.

I would work magic on a Blue Moon for something that seems unobtainable or difficult to achieve... go with the thought that whatever your intent is, the outcome might just happen 'once in a Blue Moon'.

A Blue Moon Magic Spell

You will need:
A square piece of blue fabric, felt works well. You can even decorate it with Moons if you like.
Safety pins
Paper and pen
Length of cord or ribbon, gold or silver would be good

Lay out your items and calm, ground and centre yourself.

Then make a list of all the things that you would like but you think are unobtainable, the sort of things that you think you could never achieve or own.

Once you have written your list go back over it and really think hard. Double check all of the things you wrote down. Are there some that you don't really, really want? Are there some that in reality wouldn't work for you? If there are cross them off.

Once you have narrowed down your list cut your paper into strips and write a wish on each piece. Be positive when you write each one down, and visualise it happening.

Then, using the safety pins, pin each piece of paper to the blue cloth. Once you have pinned them all fold the cloth up and tie it with the ribbon or cord.

When the Full Blue Moon is risen take the bundle outside and hold it up to her, then make your request that your wishes be fulfilled, but don't forget to thank the Goddess. You can write a poem or chant to say at this time if you wish.

Once you are done, put the bundle somewhere that you can see it regularly, on your altar would be a good place.

Then wait and see what happens...

Red Blood Moon

October's Full Moon is sometimes called the Hunter's Moon or the Blood Moon. The name comes from hunters who would track and kill their prey by the autumn moonlight, preparing their food stores for the winter.

The Red Blood Moon represents abundance, harvest and gathering, and is a time to honour the Gods and Goddesses that correspond to hunting to give thanks for the bountiful harvest and for providing for us. In magical terms this equates to workings for abundance in your life, whether it is financial or spiritual, for good health, friendships, relationships and love.

Eclipses

A lunar eclipse is a powerful time to work magic as the energies of the Moon are amplified and focused. This is a perfect time for making major transformations, releases and changes in your life.

Take some time to meditate and look at the areas of your life that need a new injection, fresh ideas and new perspectives. Also look at what blockages are keeping you from achieving your goals and dreams. Release any of the negative energy that is stopping you from following your path and focus on your new goals. Be a phoenix rising from the ashes.

If you work magic on a lunar eclipse, just remember that the power that comes with it can be a bit unpredictable. Know what you are doing and how to handle it!

Moon Diaries and Moon Time

Moon Diary

I would also encourage you to keep a Moon diary, as she is so powerful she can affect our moods, thoughts and feelings. If you chart the Moon phases and how they affect you and your emotions, you will soon begin to see a pattern emerge.

On each New Moon and Full Moon light a candle on your altar and focus on the energies.

Honouring Your Moon Time

Sorry guys, this one is more for the ladies, but if you have a lady in your life you might notice her moods change... ahem...

Society has taught us that periods are to be hated and sometimes, for some people, they can be quite physically unpleasant. However, I believe if we honour our monthly cycle we can learn to work with our bodies and hopefully lessen some of the more uncomfortable side effects that a period can bring. Having a period celebrates you being a woman; it echoes Mother Earth in the fact that a woman can create life in her own body. I have found personally, and in talking with others, that once you start following the phases of the Moon quite often your period will start to work in synch with her powers.

But the power of the Moon affecting our bodies, our emotions and our energy levels is not solely for women, it does affect men too. Although men don't have periods, the power of the Moon does play a part in moods and feelings – men can also track their moods to the Moon phases.

The Seasonal Moon

Witches celebrate eight seasonal festivals, the Sabbats, celebrating the cycles of nature and the process of growth, decay and rebirth that we are part of. Naturally, certain festivals lend themselves to being marked with a Full, Waxing or Waning Moon.

Yule is a time of rebirth, when the Sun stops retreating, stands still (the meaning of the word solstice) and begins to return.

Imbolc is when the first signs of spring growth are seen. Deep in the belly of the Earth life is stirring.

Ostara is a festival of plant fertility and marks the time when day and night are equal in length.

Beltane is a time when we celebrate human fertility, with the sacred marriage of the Earth Goddess and the Sun God.

Litha is the climax of the seasonal cycle, when the hours of daylight are longest.

Lughnasadgh is the first harvest, abundance is celebrated.

Mabon, the last harvest, and the time when the mists are rising and the veil between the worlds is becoming thin.

Samhain is when we mark the darkest time of the year, the death and decay that now must be gone through for new growth to arise.

The equinoxes and solstices are astronomical dates linked to the position of the Sun. The cross quarter festivals are dependent upon the rhythms of plants and animals. It is not hard to see that different phases of the Moon may be linked to different festivals. In fact the yearly cycle of the Sun is echoed by the monthly cycle of the Moon.

Yule for instance is associated with the New Moon and might be appropriately celebrated at this time, while Imbolc is associated with the first quarter, Beltane with pre Full Moon, Litha with Full Moon and so into the waning cycle until Samhain at the approach of Dark Moon.

As you note the phases of the Moon and their effects, you may also tune into the different times of year. The wan, shrinking Moon haunting the small hours at Samhain may look all the more melancholy because of the late autumn, while a Full Moon around Beltane may seem even more luxuriant.

The Triple Goddess

The phases of the Moon can be associated with the Triple Moon Goddess and the aspects of womanhood; the Waxing Crescent Moon being the young Maiden, full of energy and potential, then the Full Moon is the Mother aspect, the nurturer and provider, followed by the Waning Crescent and Dark Moon as the Crone, the wise woman and keeper of mysteries. They represent the cycle of life – birth, death and rebirth.

The Maiden is enchanting, new beginnings, promise, youth, pure, excitement and carefree. She is the Goddess of beauty, love and hope. She has innocence about her. Her season is spring and her colour is white.

The Mother is fertility, stability, power, fulfilment and life. She is the Goddess of love, motherhood, protection, guidance, inner peace, intuition, psychic and spiritual development and care. Her season is summer and her colour is red.

The Crone is wisdom, compassion, knowing and is full of a lifetime of experience. She is the Goddess of wisdom and experience as well as death. Her season is winter and her colour is black. She is the last stage of life, but also a reminder that the cycle never ends, life is an ever-flowing cycle. Working with the Dark Goddess teaches us that we need death as a passage to another place; it is a part of our own lifecycle.

Triple Goddess Meditation

This meditation connects you with the Maiden, Mother and Crone aspects of your own personality. Gentlemen can do the same to connect with their feminine energies or they can replace the Maiden, Mother and Crone aspects with the male counterparts, the Youth, Warrior and Sage.

Make yourself comfortable, relax and focus on your breathing. Close your eyes. Take deep breaths in...and out... Visualise the real world disappearing.

As your world dissipates you find yourself in a swirling vortex of energy. Note what colour it is, feel the peace that the energy brings you, relax and allow it to carry you. As it carries you along allow it to take any negative energies, worries or stresses from you... the energy is taking you to your inner self...

Slowly the vortex of energy disappears and you find yourself in a beautiful place. What can you see? What are your surroundings? What can you hear and what scents can you detect?

The vortex has taken you to the realm of the Triple Goddess. It is day time but you can see a Crescent Moon waxing in the sky. The landscape around you is bright and alive. You feel content and peaceful.

As you look around you see a pool of water so you make your way over. The edges of the pool have been decorated with beautiful white flowers, and the water is so inviting you slip off your clothes and submerge yourself in the water. It makes you feel alive, refreshed and renewed, you feel young and energised. This is the energy of the Maiden, of the Waxing Moon.

As you make your way out of the water you find that someone has left you fresh towels so you dry and dress. Once you have done this you look up and see a Goddess approaching, she is young and beautiful...she is YOU in your maiden form. You sit with her for a while and talk... she may have advice for you; she may have answers or a gift for you...

The Maiden Goddess now departs so you wander over to the other side of the pool where you see a small altar covered with fruit and beautiful red flowers. In the centre of the altar is a mirror. You realise that while you have been talking to the Maiden, the Moon has become full in the sky.

You stand in front of the mirror and see yourself full of life, abundance and glowing. You watch yourself change from maiden to mother, embracing all that happens. You realise someone is coming towards you and turn to see a Mother Goddess. She is strong and beautiful.

She is you in your mother phase; she sits and talks with you and reminds you about the qualities of the mother within yourself, nurturing and caring but also reminds you not to neglect yourself and your own well-being. Talk with her, listen to her and accept any advice or gifts she gives you. She is the life force. When you are finished she departs.

You realise that the Moon in the sky has now turned into a Waning Crescent. You look around and see a crossroads, at the side of it sits a Crone Goddess beside her cauldron so you make your way over to her. She asks you to sit with her. She is a crone, but still beautiful. She is you in your crone phase, the Dark Mother, the wise woman.

Sit and talk with her, ask her questions, listen to her advice. She will ask you to acknowledge yourself as your own source of wisdom and power. Leave behind any doubts or insecurities of the Maiden, the emotional aspects of the Mother and find the centre of yourself, the core, the part of you that connects with spirit. The Crone Goddess asks you to acknowledge the dark side of you.

When you are ready you get up and thank the Crone Goddess then make your way back past the altar and then past the pool.

As you do so you feel the vortex of swirling energy take hold of you again, this time it brings you back to your own reality. Stamp your feet and wriggle your fingers to bring yourself back fully.

Moon Names

Each monthly Moon also has its own name. If you notice, each Moon name usually relates to the weather, the region, the culture, the season or an animal – these names reflect what was happening at the time of year for the native people. Each monthly Moon will also have its own specific magical properties and correspondences.

January
Wolf Moon, Quiet Moon, Snow Moon, Cold Moon, Chaste Moon, Disting Moon and Moon of Little Winter.

Work magic for beginnings, protection, personal issues, aiming for goals, hidden agendas and reversing spells.

February
Ice Moon, Storm Moon, Horning Moon, Hunger Moon, Wild Moon, Red and Cleansing Moon, Quickening Moon, Solmonath and Big Winter Moon.

Work magic for purification, healing, growth, responsibility, forgiveness, love of yourself and new plans.

March
Storm Moon, Seed Moon, Moon of Winds, Plow Moon, Worm Mon, Herthmonath, Lentzinmanoth, Lenting Moon, Sap Moon, Crow Moon and Moon of the Snowblind.

Work magic for prosperity, exploration, new beginnings, balance, truth, honesty and clarity in a situation.

April
Growing Moon, Hare Moon, Seed or Planting Moon, Planters' Moon, Budding Trees Moon, Eastermonath, Ostarmanoth, Pink Mon, Green Grass Moon.

Work magic for creativity, balance, change, confidence, opportunities, emotions and productivity.

May

Hare Moon, Merry Moon, Dyad Moon, Flower Moon, Frogs Return Moon, Thrilmilcmonath, Sproutkale, Winnemanoth, Planting Moon and Moon When the Ponies Shed.

Work magic for creativity, intuition, faerie magic, tree and plant magic, psychic work and spirit connections.

June

Mead Moon, Moon of Horses, Lovers Moon, Strong Sun Moon, Honey Moon, Aerra Litha, Brachmanoth, Strawberry Moon, Rose Moon and Moon of Making Fat

Work magic for protection, strength, decisions, responsibility, personal issues and inner power.

July

Hay Moon, Wort Moon, Moon of Claiming, Moon of Blood, Blessing Moon, Maedmonat, Hewimanoth, Fallow Moon, Buck Moon and Thunder Moon.

Work magic for relaxation, preparation, success, dreams, divination, new plans, reaching your goals and spiritual work.

August

Corn Moon, Barley Moon, Dispute Moon, Wedmonath, Harvest Moon and Moon When Cherries Turn Black.

Work magic for harvesting projects, reaping what you sow, appreciation, health, good friendships and abundance.

September

Harvest Moon, Wine Moon, Singing Moon, Sturgeon Moon, Haligmonath, Witumanoth and Moon When Deer Paw the Earth.

Work magic for balance, organisation, cleansing, mental and

spiritual clearing out and finding peace.

October

Blood Moon, Harvest Moon, Hunter's Moon, Shedding Moon, Winterfelleth, Windermanoth, Falling Leaf Moon, Ten Colds Moon and Moon of the Changing Seasons.

Work magic for divination, spirit contact, death and rebirth, justice, balance, harmony and letting go of that which does not serve your higher good.

November

Snow Moon, Dark Moon, Fog Moon, Beaver Moon, Mourning Moon, Blotmanoth, Herbistmanoth, Mad Moon, Moon of Storms and Moon when deer shed antlers.

Work magic for transformation, preparation, strength, communication with the divine and inner work.

December

Cold Moon, Oak Moon, Wolf Moon, Moon of Long Nights, Long Nights Moon, Aerra Geola, Wintermonat, Heilagmanoth, Big Winter Moon and Moon of Popping Trees.

Work magic for death and rebirth, balance, spiritual matters, family, friendships, relationships, shadow work and personal issues.

Celtic Tree Calendar

I am not sure how old the Celtic Tree calendar is. Some say it is as ancient as the Ogham, some say it is a more modern invention by author Robert Graves. However, it is a lovely calendar to follow and is based on thirteen months, each named for trees, all based on the Ogham. My own coven uses the Full Moon of each of the tree months for our ritual celebrations.

Beth (Birch) December 24 to January 20
A time of rebirth and regeneration, new projects and new endeavours. It is a time to look towards the light again and a time of change.

Luis (Rowan) January 21 to February 17
This Moon is associated with the Goddess Brighid. It is a good time of year to perform initiations or self-dedications. It represents intuition, protection and inner vision.

Nion (Ash) February 18 to March 17
The Ash is the World Tree, Yggdrasil. This is a month for working inner magic and spiritual journeys. It is a good time to connect with the energies of all the worlds, seen and unseen.

Fearn (Alder) March 18 to April 14
Alder is a tree of balance and for action from inspiration. This is a good month for working divination and with prophecies as well as for boosting your own intuition.

Saille (Willow) April 15 to May 12
Willow is a tree of healing and protection. It can help us to connect with our emotions and bring us inner strength.

Uath (Hawthorn) May 13 to June 9

This Moon month is about fertility, male energy and fire. The hawthorn is good for protection and is said to grow by the entrances to the faerie world.

Duir (Oak) June 10 to July 7

Such a powerful and strong tree, Oak brings the magical energies of inner strength and courage. This is a good month for working strength and protection spells along with any prosperity ones too.

Tinne (Holly) July 8 to August 4

Holly is a tree of balance, luck and protection. The tree can help with restoring direction and bringing balance into your life as well as helping with emotional situations.

Coll (Hazel) August 5 to September 1

This is the Jedi tree ;-) It carries with it the magical energies to help you tap into the life force that is within you. It is all about creativity and inspiration to bring about good changes.

Muin (Vine) September 2 to September 29

Grapes! Which means harvest, so this month is all about reaping what you have sown. This is a good month for re-gaining balance and bringing happiness and passion into your life.

Gort (Ivy) September 30 to October 27

Ivy reminds us of the circle of life, that death means rebirth. This is a good time of year to get rid of any negativity from your life; a time to make improvements.

Ngetal (Reed) October 28 to November 24

Yep, I know a reed isn't technically a tree! Reed is connected with the Underworld and those souls that have passed. The Reed

Moon is a good time for scrying and divination and working with spirit guides.

Ruis (Elder) November 25 to December 23

A time of endings and new beginnings, of death and rebirth. Elder is a kind of phoenix tree to enable you to rise from the ashes. It is a time of regeneration and brings with it wisdom and understanding.

Moon Deities

There are thousands and thousands of different deities all with different energies and personalities, some of them are specifically aligned with Moon magic. The list below shows a small selection of them but it is by no means comprehensive.

Alignak: An Inuit God of the Moon and the weather, he also controls the tides, earthquakes and eclipses.

Andraste: An ancient British Goddess said to have been worshipped by Queen Boadicea and connected to the Moon. She is a goddess of war, but in her light aspect she rules love and fertility. Her animals are the raven and the hare.

Anuket: Egyptian Goddess of the Crescent Moon, agriculture and the Nile. She also looks after the poor. Her symbols are shells, coins and fish.

Arianrhod: Welsh Goddess of the Dark Moon, the stars, the sea, reincarnation, prophecy, dreams and the future. Her name means silver disc or wheel. She is part of the triple goddess triad with Blodeuwedd and Cerridwen. She is able to shapeshift into an owl. She receives the souls of the dead and guides them on. She is also one of the five goddesses of Avalon (along with Blodeuwedd, Branwen, Cerridwen and Rhiannon).

Artemis: Greek Goddess of the hunt and associated with the Crescent Moon. Her twin brother, Apollo, is associated with the Sun, so she gradually became a Moon goddess as a balance. She also rules forests, woodlands and wild animals and defends the weak and the young. Her symbols are the bow and arrow, the deer and the bear.

Artimpaasa: Scythian Goddess of the Moon and the tides. She also rules love and family relations.

Athene: Greek goddess of weaving, which is often a trait associated with the Moon. Athene is also Goddess of Wisdom and one of the three Greek virgin goddesses. She protects and defends and is also a philosopher. Her symbols are the owl and the olive tree.

Auchimalgen: A South American Moon Goddess. She is the spirit of compassion. She looks after the human race, protecting them and keeping evil away.

Bendis: Thracian Moon Goddess often associated with Artemis and Hecate. She is Goddess of hunting, mysteries, orgies, athletes and the Moon.

Blodeuwedd: A Welsh Goddess with a connection to both the Moon and death and reincarnation (aspects of the Dark Moon). She is the maiden of the Triple Goddess triad (with Arianrhod and Cerridwen). She is the May Queen, Goddess of spring, flowers and initiations. She is also known for her betrayal and manipulation.

Cerridwen: Welsh Goddess associated with the Full Moon. She is also Goddess of wisdom, inspiration and intuition. Keeper of the sacred cauldron in which she brews the 'awen', she represents spiritual transformation and justice. She covers all three aspects of the Triple Goddess, but also forms the triad with Blodeuwedd and Arianrhod. She rules prophecy and magic, death and rebirth. Her animal is the white sow.

Ch'ang-O: Chinese Moon Goddess. Ch'ang-O and her husband were banished from the upper world to live as mortals. She wanted to return so drank an immortality potion meant for both of them, which sent her floating up to the Moon where she is now destined to spend eternity. Her symbols are incense, sweet food and the hare.

Coyolxauhqui: An Aztec Goddess whose name means 'golden bells'. She died in the womb, killed by her brother who cut off her head and threw it up to the sky, where she now remains… as the Moon. She is often depicted as a beautiful maiden wearing clothes decorated with lunar images and bells.

Cybele: A Roman Underworld Goddess who is associated with the Dark Moon. She is mother of the Gods, fertility and nature. She also protects from war and invasion.

Demeter: Goddess of the Full Moon, the harvest and agriculture. She is the Mother aspect of the Triple Goddess triad with Persephone and Hecate. Her symbol is a cornucopia. She always looks after those in need.

Diana: A Roman goddess of the hunt, woodlands, forests and the Moon and Queen of the Witches. She is very beautiful, controls magic and protects women. She looks after all animals, those in slavery and the poor.

Ereshkigal: A Sumerian Goddess who was called Queen of the Underworld and in her aspect as the Crone is Goddess of the Dark Moon. She not only represents the dark and that which is unseen, but also the shadow of our personalities.

Freyja: Although not called a Moon Goddess, many of her attributes connect her with both the Full and Dark Moons. She is Goddess of love and war and a beautiful Maiden Goddess. She represents love, family, sensuality, souls of the dead and poetry.

Gleti: A Moon Goddess from West Africa, she is the mother of the stars and the planets ruling love and light. Her husband is the Sun God.

Hecate: The oldest Greek form of the Triple Goddess. She is connected to childbirth and maidenhood so has all aspects of the Moon phases, but is often connected to the Dark Moon as she represents magic, ghosts and the spirit world. Her powers cover Heaven, Earth and the Underworld; she is protector of the spirit world and associated with crossroads.

Imatar: The Finnish-Ugrian Goddess of the Crescent Moon

Inanna of Sumeria: Also known as Ishtar in Babylon, Goddess of love and war, Queen of Heaven and Earth and the Full Moon, she is seen as the stars. Inanna is also Goddess of seduction, sensuality, fertility, mating, wisdom and the magic of life and death. Her war Goddess side protects her followers. Her symbols are the eight pointed star and the lion.

Ix Chel: A Mayan Moon Goddess and mother of the Mayan deities, she rules life and death. She covers all aspects of womanhood from maiden to crone and represents creativity, inspiration, weaving, artists and musicians.

Maat: Egyptian Goddess of justice, order, truth, balance, law and the Crescent Moon. She measures the soul with her feather of truth to decide whether it goes to the land of the dead or is destroyed.

Mama Quilla/Mama Killa, Quillamama: Incan Goddess of time and the Full Moon. She keeps time flowing and is keeper of the calendar. She also protects married women.

Marama: Maori Moon Goddess from New Zealand. She is a Goddess of light and resurrection, collecting the souls of the dead and making sure they travel onwards away from the living.

Manidroe: A Norse God, son of Mundilfore, he rode the chariot of the Moon.

Mawu: From West Africa, this Goddess rules the Moon and the night she brings with her wisdom and embodies motherhood. She has a twin consort, Liza, who is a Sun God. Her symbol is the cowrie shell.

Neith: Egyptian Goddess of women, marriage, war, hunting, weaving and the Crescent Moon.

Nephthys: Egyptian Goddess of the dead, darkness, the mysteries of death and the Dark Moon. A powerful goddess, she protects souls, has great magical power, is Queen of the Underworld and offers rebirth.

Pajau Yan: Vietnamese goddess of health, healing and the Moon. She gives good fortune to the living and helps the dead to the underworld, she resides within the Moon.

Pasiphae: A three-faced Moon Goddess from Crete, a powerful witch and oracle. She also rules the Sun.

Parvati: Indian Goddess of feminine energies, womanhood, patience, artists, dancers, poets and the Crescent Moon. She is the Maiden from the Triple Goddess triad which includes Durga and Kali Ma.

Selene: A Greek Goddess of Moon magic, sleep, dreams, prophecy. Her brother is Helios, a Greek Sun God.

Sina: A Polynesian Goddess who lives within the Moon and protects night travellers. She travelled to the Moon in her canoe and loved it so much that she stayed!

Thoth: An Egyptian Moon God, he also represents magic and wisdom.

Venus: Roman Goddess of love, sex, beauty and is associated with the Full Moon. She removes trouble and anguish and brings joy and happiness; she is also the Goddess of prostitutes.

Vesta: Roman Goddess of hearth, home, fire, domesticity, family and the Crescent Moon.

Yemaya: African Goddess of water, the sea, feminine energies, women, pregnancy, birth, healing and the Moon.

Meditation to Meet a Moon Deity

Relax and make yourself comfortable, close your eyes and focus on your breathing, deep breaths in … and out… Visualise the real world disappearing.

As your world dissipates you find yourself in a stone building, as you turn around and take in your surroundings you realise you are in a courtyard with stone pillars all around you and beneath your feet is a beautiful mosaic floor.

You turn your head upwards and realise that the stone building has no roof and you can see the dark, indigo blue night sky. It is full of twinkling stars and a beautiful Moon shines its light into the centre of the courtyard.

You notice at one end of the courtyard there is a stone seat covered in cushions so you head towards it and make yourself comfortable.

Once you are seated you can take in the details of your surroundings. The pillars around the courtyard are painted with many wonderful lunar symbols and signs.

You then hear movement and look to see a figure heading towards you from across the courtyard. As they come into focus, what do they look like? What are they wearing? They come right over and sit beside you.

This is your opportunity to ask them any questions that you wish to. Spend as much time as you need to in conversation.

When you are ready, the deity hugs you and departs, with your thanks.

Make your way back to the courtyard entrance and back to this reality, stamp your feet and wriggle your fingers.

Magic to Honour the Moon

Make a Moon Altar

You could set up an altar to honour the phases of the Moon and the dark mysteries of the night. It doesn't have to be large, just a small shelf or corner of a sideboard. Go with your instincts (as always!) on what items to put on your altar, but here are some suggestions to get you started:

Candles: Change the colour for each different phase of the Moon. (I would suggest white for waxing, red for full and black for waning to represent the three phases of the Triple Goddess.) Or you could use white or silver candles for the Moon and darker ones for the night such as deep red, forest green, purple or dark blue.

Herbs, crystals, shells, bowl of water: Use crystals that symbolise the Moon phases or the night. Night crystals might be apache tears, obsidian, angelite, celestite, smokey quartz, fluorite, quartz, jet, blue beryl, moonstone, selenite, pearl, opal, onyx, sodalite, dark agates, aquamarine and mother of pearl.

Moon Power Animals

Place pictures of animal totems on your altar that correspond with the Moon or the night-time. These are generally nocturnal creatures but you may find you connect with others, go with what shows itself to you. Some Moon power animal suggestions are:

Bat: (That's an obvious one isn't it?) Bat medicine includes avoiding obstacles, barriers, transformation, releasing bad habits and personality traits, learning from past lives, journeying, intuition, understanding dreams, illusion and communication.

Cat: Cat medicine includes curiosity (of course!), love, mystery, independence, healing, magic, mystery, seeing the unseen, dreams, protection, feminine energies, intuition, telepathy, self-acceptance, fertility and foresight.

Jaguar: Jaguar medicine includes reclaiming your power, aggression, power, lunar energies, multi-tasking, solitary, clairaudience, inner visions, intuition, guide, teacher, mentor and magic.

Black Panther: Black panther medicine includes pacing yourself, fast response, meeting deadlines, depth of vision, psychic sight, inner knowing, passion, sensuality, feminine powers, the dark mother, the Dark Moon, power of the night, death and rebirth, cunning, strength, boldness, beauty, astral travel and otherworld journeying.

Moth: Moth medicine includes working with shadow, transformation, metamorphosis, ability to find light in the dark, hearing the unspoken word, psychic abilities, healing, optimism, letting go of negative energies and moving forward.

Owl: Owl medicine includes silent and swift movement, keen sight, unmasking deceit, an excellent underworld guide, wisdom, magic, darkness, freedom, dreams, shapeshifting, clairvoyance, astral projection, messages, finding the hidden truth, secrets and omens.

Wolf: Wolf medicine includes teaching, individuality, shape shifting, group consciousness, loyalty, devotion, talent, ritual, attention to detail, security, guardians, spirituality, truth, family, Moon energies, emotions, trust and intuition.

Cow and Bull: The bull symbolises fertility while the cow is a symbol of motherhood and nourishment. The cow is a very lunar energy while the bull symbolises the Sun, although his horns are in the shape of the Crescent Moon. The bull is earth, possessions, the mundane, the union of male and female, production, sowing new seeds, stubbornness, insensitivity, asserting your feminine energies and insecurity. Defending your family, being content, being aware of your surroundings, being alert, being conscientious and strong are all cow and bull medicine.

Crow: Crow medicine includes change, movement, mystery, illusion, the hidden and sacred, interpretation, trickery, symbols, omens, dreams, shadow work, hidden opportunities, shapeshifting, clairvoyance, intuition, introspection, wisdom, integrity, being mindful, truth, standards, change, the past, the future, messages, magic, opportunities, deception, unseen forces, light and dark and spiritual strength.

Dog: Dog medicine includes loyalty, devotion, protection, friendship, companionship, faithfulness, team spirit, dedication, communication, strength, stamina, hunting, retrieving, guardians, law, order and the underworld.

Dragon: The types and breeds of dragon are numerous and a whole book could be written on them alone. However, as a general guide, dragon medicine includes power, transformation, infinity, wisdom, the supernatural, change and guidance.

Hare: (Definitely a Moon animal, think 'moongazy'.) Hare medicine includes transformation, hidden teachings, intuition, messages, quick thinking, protection, fertility, not worrying about the future and Moon gazing.

Raven: Raven medicine includes introspection, courage, self-knowledge, magic, healing, creation, rebirth, secrets, shape shifting, respect, shifting consciousness, will, intention, mysteries, changes, spiritual awakening, inner work, transformation and mysticism.

Snake: Snake medicine includes fertility, healing, death, the otherworld, sexuality, sensuality, magic, mystery, rebirth, reincarnation, immortality, spirit, guardianship, protection, change, creativity, psychic energy, wisdom, understanding and connection with spirit.

Meditation to Meet your Night Totem/Guardian

Relax and make yourself comfortable. Close your eyes. Focus on your breathing, deep breaths in...and out... Visualise the real world disappearing.

As your world dissipates you find yourself in a field, it is dusk and you smell the scent of the night air.

As you turn around and take in your surroundings the scene takes your breath away. On the horizon ahead of you is the ancient sacred site of Stonehenge, the stones penetrating the sky line.

You make your way towards the stones...

As you reach the outer stones you reach up and place your hands on one of them. Feel the deep, powerful Earth energy...

When you are ready, head to the centre of the stone circle and sit yourself down on the ground. Ask for your night totem to make itself known to you...

Sit quietly and watch the land, the stones and the sky... see what animal comes to you...

When a creature appears, see if you can communicate with them (don't worry if you don't meet an animal this time, sometimes it can take several attempts).

When you are ready, thank your night guide and know that when you need to connect with its energies again, it will come to you.

Make your way back out of the stone circle and back across the field.

Slowly come back to this reality, stamp your feet and wriggle your fingers.

Drawing Down the Moon

Most witches will have heard of, or experienced the rite called Drawing Down the Moon (you can draw down the Sun too). This ritual supposedly dates back to the Dianic witches of Thessaly from ancient Greece. It is a powerful ritual and can lead to a very moving experience that can shed light on every aspect of your life and inner being. It can also open up your psychic abilities. This is my interpretation of the Drawing Down the Moon ritual, there are more structured and ceremonial versions that can be found on the internet if you prefer. It is the art of drawing upon the power of the Moon to send you into a trance and to channel the power of the Goddess. In some covens or traditions, the High Priestess will say the Charge of the Goddess (the original was attributed to Doreen Valiente); to invoke her, I am sharing here a version of the Charge of the Goddess written by Lesley Lightbody:

Diana, Istarte, Kali-Maa
Athena, Rhiannon, Ishtar
Names forgotten, names remembered
As the Old ways are now honoured

Mother Goddess come hear our call
As we rejoice in the Spirit of the All
Invoking your name three times three
As we have great need of thee

Gathered round the sacred pyre
Woods are burned upon the hour
Sacred woods your numbers nine
We honour those forgotten by time

The Divine Mother resides in us all
But only some will answer the call
Seekers of knowledge search without
Within the answers are found without a doubt

Protector of the Forest Glen
Protector of animals and of men
As old as time, as ancient as space
Cast your circle, make a Sacred place

Honour the Mother, honour the Moon
The circle of life, the natures boon
Call Her name, She'll answer the prayer
Maiden, Mother or Crone with matted hair

By many names the Mother has been known
Her legends increase, her stories roam
A thousand names Our Lady has it's true
A cosmic keeper of the green and blue

Blessed are we that know her name
Blessed are we that feel no shame
Blessed are we to hear Her call
And honour the Goddess as our all

This ritual really needs to be performed outside as you need to be able to see the Moon, the Full Moon is preferable. Even if the sky is full of clouds, the power of the Full Moon will still be available to you.

Cast a circle and call the quarters as you would do for any ritual. Then slowly start breathing in the light of the Moon, filling your entire body with its beams. Make sure you do a bit of grounding through your feet to stop yourself from floating away though!

The purpose is to go into trance to enable the Goddess to channel through you. This can be done by invocations to her, but I find that starting to slowly spin myself around, swirling and twirling whilst trying to keep an eye on the Moon works well. When you come to a stop the Moon seems to rush down towards you. As the power of the Moon enters your body you may get images or hear messages, these may be for you, but if you are in a group the messages may be for other members of the ritual. Speak out loud everything you hear and see, whether it is words, symbols or images.

When the messages have stopped you can kneel on the ground and have a scrying bowl filled with water in front of you. Make sure the moonlight shines directly onto the water, you may then also get more images in the surface of the water.

When you have finished and closed your ritual, make sure to ground properly.

You may want to write down all the messages as soon as you finish as they do have a tendency to escape from your memory quite quickly!

In a coven it is generally the High Priestess who draws down the Moon, but it can also work very well with several members at the same time.

Astrological Moon Signs

Everyone, even those people who aren't even remotely interested in astrology, will probably know their horoscope sign. Although referred to as a 'star sign' it is actually your Sun sign and as everyone was born under one… you are also born under a Moon sign.

We are familiar with the Zodiac and the cycle that the Sun makes through its signs, but the Moon (and all the planets) also travels through them. The Moon passes through each entire sign in just over two days. The Moon's passage through the Zodiac signs takes slightly less than 28 days. There are 13 of these cycles in a year. This means that the Full Moon appears in a different sign of the Zodiac each month. The Moon is always opposite the Sun when it is full, so if you know what sign the Sun is occupying, the Full Moon will be in the opposite sign of the Zodiac. (The Moon moves faster than the Sun).

If you can work your magic when the Moon is in a specific sign of the Zodiac it will add a lot of power to the working. If you add to that the correct Moon phase then you will have huge amounts of oomph!

Aries

General: Action, taking risks, independence. For bringing in energy and enthusiasm to your plans or new ventures. Expression, self reliance, enthusiasm and spontaneity.

Watch out for impulses, impatience, lack of energy and organisation and tempers.

New Moon: Confidence, learning, fear and anger control, new projects and taking risks.

Full Moon: Social situations, romance, music, honour.

Element: Fire.

Colours: Red.

Incense: Cinnamon, basil, nettle, chervil, ginseng, pine, ginger, wormwood, geranium.

Aries Incense Blend: Equal parts of cedar, ginseng, basil and pine with a few drops of ginger essential oil.

Taurus

General: Practical matters, permanence, sex, financial security, prosperity, confidence to speak out, growth of any kind, stability, peace, affection, devotion and harmony, staying power, bringing love into your life. Watch out for greed, stubbornness, possessiveness and wanting to have your own way!

New Moon: Prosperity, harmony, investing, long term goals, love, healing and peace.

Full Moon: Success, money, serenity and investments.

Element: Earth.

Colours: Pale to medium blue, green, pink, rose, mauve, burnt orange.

Incense: Benzoin, mint, thyme, violet, marsh mallow, mugwort, vervain, catnip. Taurus Incense Blend: Equal parts of mugwort, vervain and thyme with a few drops of benzoin essential oil.

Gemini

General: Playing with ideas, learning, intellect, multi-tasking, communicating (although this is not good for permanent changes), short-distance travel, business communication, deals and transactions, sorting out disputes.

Watch out for manipulation, lack of focus, disorganisation and back stabbing.

New Moon: Learning, research, balance, meditation, divination, learning, family matters, clearing out the old and moving onto the new.

Full Moon: Magic, messages, healing and religion.

Element: Air.

Colours: Blue, yellow, violet.

Incense: Lavender, dill, parsley, anise, rosemary, sage, lemon grass, marjoram.

Gemini Incense Blend: Equal parts of lemon grass, sage and lavender with a few drops of rosemary essential oil.

Cancer

General: Home, children and family (but watch for others' sensitivities), motherhood, pregnancy, finding a new home, exploration of past lives, scrying, divination, finding household decorations that you would like, emotions, psychic work, protection and sympathy.

Watch out for mood swings, finding fault in others, irritability, judging others and dwelling on the negative.

New Moon: Feminine matters, peace, protection, psychic skills, dreams, divination, drawing positive energy, pregnancy and emotions.

Full Moon: Stability, home and family matters.

Element: Water.

Colours: white, silver.

Incense: Damiana, sage, aloe, feverfew, heather, myrrh, chamomile, lemon balm, bay, parsley.

Cancer Incense Blend: Equal parts of chamomile, feverfew, heather and myrrh with a few drops of myrrh essential oil.

Leo

General: Vitality, the heart, strong feelings, entertainment, opportunity, fertility, confidence, courage, strength, kindness, leadership abilities, bringing money to you (but only if it is badly needed).

Watch out for selfishness, arrogance, stubbornness and bullying.

New Moon: Courage, strength, positive thinking, success, loyalty, talents, having fun and generosity.

Full Moon: Humanitarian issues, personal goals and groups.

Element: Fire.

Colours: Gold, deep yellow, bright orange.

Incense: Frankincense, sunflower, lemon balm, chamomile, tarragon, cinnamon, orange, ginger, eyebright.

Leo Incense Blend: Equal parts of dried orange peel, cinnamon stick and frankincense with a few drops of ginger oil.

Virgo

General: Organisation, detail, health, reaping your just rewards, fitness, refining your diet, purification, acquiring or improving skills, ensuring a good 'harvest' from a project, analysis, logical choices, precision and solutions.

Watch out for criticism, arguments, control and lack of trust.

New Moon: Problem solving, information, choices, accuracy, inner work and finding mistakes.

Full Moon: Problem solving, intuition and divination.

Element: Earth.

Colours: Grey, green, black.

Incense: Lemongrass, caraway, fennel, bergamot, dill, mint, horehound, marjoram.

Virgo Incense Blend: Equal parts of fennel, mint and marjoram with a few drops of bergamot essential oil.

Libra

General: Contracts, partnership, love, beauty, cooperation, courtesy, charm, eloquence, friendships, bringing balance and harmony into your relationships, marriage, business contracts and agreements, legal matters, justice, increasing your social life, attracting love into your life.

Watch out for judging others, unreliability, changeable attitude and a bit of chaos.

New Moon: The arts, love, friendship, romance, cooperation, communication and partnerships.

Full Moon: Social situations, decisions and justice.

Element: Air.

Colours: Pink, pale green, mauve, light blue.

Incense: Rose, catnip, elderberry, thyme, St. John's Wort, lavender, mint, benzoin, bergamot.

Libra Incense Blend: Equal parts of lavender, mint and thyme with a few drops of benzoin essential oil.

Scorpio

General: Loyalty, ownership (but watch out for suspicion and anger), matters requiring insight, increasing your libido or to attract passionate love (be careful though as relationships with a Scorpio influence are likely to be transformational and not always predictable!), healing of the mind and emotions, scrying, concentration, single mindedness, rebirth, transformation, wisdom, karma and instinct.

Watch out for secrets, lies, jealousy, and suspicion, lack of forgiveness, grudges and hate.

New Moon: Power, transformation, karma, instincts, clarity, wisdom, stop gossip, emotions, endings, death, rebirth and past life work.

Full Moon: Energy, resources and transformation.

Element: Water.

Colours: Deep red.

Incense: Basil, sage, catnip, coriander, sandalwood, thyme, nettle.

Scorpio Incense Blend: Equal parts of sandalwood, thyme and sage with a few drops of coriander essential oil.

Sagittarius

General: Philosophy, adventure, journeys, study, honesty, imagination, long-distance travel, learning, writing and publishing, religion and philosophy, generosity, faith, understanding, hope and optimism.

Watch out for no loyalty or commitment, emotional withdrawal, shifting blame and irresponsibility.

New Moon: Projects, talents, understanding, hope, faith, awareness and travel.

Full Moon: Knowledge and communication.

Element: Fire.

Colours: Purple, royal blue.

Incense: Cedar wood, sage, basil, borage, saffron, nutmeg, sandalwood, chervil.

Sagittarius Incense Blend: Equal parts of sage, nutmeg and cedar wood with a few drops of sandalwood essential oil.

Capricorn

General: Building, rules and regulations, discipline (this could be depressing), career matters, ambition, determination, spiritual matters, structure, self-discipline, sincerity and organisation.

Watch out for pessimism, anxiety, feelings of failure and self-pity.

New Moon: Authority, schools, savings, justice, promotion, order, self-discipline and sciences.

Full Moon: Home, school and magical restructuring.

Element: Earth.

Colours: Black, dark green, dark blue, indigo.

Incense: Myrrh, rosemary, tarragon, caraway, chamomile, mullein, patchouli, comfrey, Solomon's seal, marjoram.

Capricorn Incense Blend: Equal parts of myrrh, rosemary and marjoram with a few drops of patchouli oil.

Aquarius

General: Inventions, social life, future goals, technology, science, forming and maintaining friendships, establishing groups, gaining more freedom or autonomy (be careful of bringing in rebellious energies though), developing intuition, independence, heightened perception and resourcefulness, becoming more detached or overcoming being too emotional.

Watch out for unorganised thoughts, selfishness, not finishing projects and being opinionated.

New Moon: Independence, change, love, new ideas, individuality and the sciences.

Full Moon: Courage, loyalty, leadership, self-worth and independence.

Element: Air.

Colours: Electric blue.

Incense: Eucalyptus, comfrey, rosemary, fennel, pine, clover, fenugreek, broom, violet, valerian.

Aquarius Incense Blend: Equal parts pine, rosemary and fennel with a few drops of clover essential oil.

Pisces

General: Spiritual and psychic matters (but guard against confusion and deception), creativity, the arts, care, compassion, peace, devotion, inspiration and empathy, enhance or develop psychic abilities, letting life flow.

Watch out for discontent, emotional imbalance, secrets, depression and lack of concentration.

New Moon: Imagination, visualisation, dream work, divination, compassion, peace, seeing the big picture.

Full Moon: Dream work, meditation and helping others.

Element: Water.

Colours: Sea green, sea blue, misty grey, pearly mauves and blues.

Incense: Sage, basil, lemon balm, lemon, orris root, elder, borage.

Pisces Incense Blend: Equal parts lemon balm, dried lemon peel and orris root with a few drops of lemon essential oil.

Moon Symbols

There are many symbols and signs associated with the Moon, the animal totem ones we have covered earlier, but we can add to that:

Boats: Egyptians used carved sky boats as symbols of the Moon and the Babylonians called the Moon the Boat of Light.

Circle: The Full Moon is often represented as a simple line drawing circle and, of course, her shape is that too. Some ancient stone circles may also have been built to represent the shape of the moon.

Crescent: The Waxing and Waning Moons are often depicted as a crescent shape (one either side of a circle to show the triple moon). Tip the crescent shape on its side and you also have the horns of the God and this shape can also be seen in a lot of ancient Moon deity headdresses.

Dew: Drops of dew are often associated with the Moon, washing your face in early morning dew after a Full Moon is said to bring you beauty.

Eye: The eye is very often used in Ancient Egyptian art as a representation of the Moon.

Fish: The fish is sometimes used as a symbol of the Moon, possibly connected to mermaids.

Frog: This creatures is often associated with the Moon.

Grotto: A sacred space that contains a Moon tree where Moon deities were worshipped.

Horns: As previously mentioned, the crescent shape made by bull horns has connections with the Moon going back throughout history.

Horseshoe: Associated with luck but also the Moon due to its crescent shape.

Hounds: Dark hounds have often been connected with the dark energies of the Moon.

Mirror: Round-shaped mirrors are often representative of the Moon.

Pomegranate: With its red flesh and juice wrapped around the seeds, the pomegranate is not only a symbol of the dead but also of the Moon.

Sickle: Associated with the Moon due to its crescent shape again, but this time in the form of a sickle, which is often carried by druids.

Shell: I associate shells with water and emotions and that also links in with the energies of the Moon. I have a large round flat shell on my altar to symbolise the Full Moon.

Silver: Silver is a metal that has often been connected with the Moon. Maybe it is due to the colour, the alchemy or the magical properties or both.

Spiral: Think of the way a spiral works going up and down or in and out, this also echoes the phases of the Moon.

Well: Another connection between water and the Moon.

Willow Tree: A sacred Moon tree.

Wings: The Moon (and the Sun) are sometimes depicted with wings. I think this also has a connection to angels.

Yin and Yang: The Chinese symbol for balance and duality could also represent the light and the dark phases of the Moon.

The Moon at Home

You can bring the power of the Moon into your home by using ornaments and decorations. They don't have to be expensive, be creative!

Colours are a good place to start. The obvious ones are silver and, of course, white, but white and pale blue are good too along with pale greens and even lilacs. That could mean the colour of your walls, cushions, throws or candles. You could add in silver or crystal ornaments or bowls as well. The obvious ones are pictures and images of the Moon and the night sky as well as images of the Goddess.

White flowers work well too, along with incense and oils that have scents that correspond to the Moon phases.

Any water ideas can bring lunar energy into your home, such as a fish tank or one of the little indoor fountains that you can get or even shells to represent water.

Have fun with it!

Planting with the Moon

A lot of gardeners, even those who aren't witches, plant and harvest by the phases of the Moon. You can still find old almanacs that list what to plant and when in line with astrological timings. Think how much the Moon affects the sea and her tides, so it must affect the earth and how things grow too.

A Waxing Moon is good for planting. Fruit ready for eating straight away should be picked on a Waxing Moon; a Waning Moon is good for planting plants that fruit below ground such as potatoes. A Waning Moon is also good for pruning, weeding and harvesting food to be stored.

Just after a New Moon plant leafy vegetables and herb seeds.

Waxing Moon gardening activities include potting cuttings, re-pottting house plants and picking herbs, fruit and vegetables for eating straight away.

On a Full Moon plant vegetables such as tomatoes, peppers and onions (any type of 'watery' vegetables and fruit). Fertilise your plants on a Full Moon too.

Just after Full Moon plant tuber vegetables such as carrots and potatoes, also biennials and perennials.

On a waning Moon start a compost heap, weed, cut and prune, pick fruits and flowers, herbs and vegetables that will be stored.

Close to the Dark Moon cut timber and spray any fruit trees (preferably with eco friendly spray).

Then you have the categories for the astrological signs; a list of each type of energy is show below, either barren, productive, semi-fruitful or fruitful:

Moon in Aries: Barren
Moon in Taurus: Productive
Moon in Gemini: Barren

Moon in Cancer: Fruitful
Moon in Leo: Barren
Moon in Virgo: Barren
Moon in Libra: Semi fruitful
Moon in Scorpio: Fruitful
Moon in Sagittarius: Barren
Moon in Capricorn: Productive
Moon in Aquarius: Barren
Moon in Pisces: Fruitful

Another useful guide is:

Above Soil-Level Plants: These are the plants that will produce crops above the ground; these should be sown the day after the New Moon up until the first quarter, preferably in a fertile or semi-fertile astrological sign.

Annuals: Plant the day after the New Moon up until the day before the first quarter, preferably in a fertile or semi-fertile astrological sign.

Below Soil-Level Plants: These are the plants that crop under the ground. These should be planted during the day after the Full Moon, preferably in a fertile or semi-fertile astrological sign.

Biennials and Perennials: This category includes shrubs and trees. Begin planting the day after the Full Moon and up to the day before the last quarter preferably in a fertile or semi-fertile astrological sign.

Seed Collection: This is best done at the Full Moon when the Moon is in a fire or air astrological sign such as Aries, Leo, Sagittarius, Libra, Gemini or Aquarius.

Harvesting: Picking fresh flowers and smaller harvests for magical use straight away, can be done in the early evening. If you want to dry and store the flowers and herbs, cut them mid morning, after the dew has evaporated. Fruit and vegetables are best harvested during the Waning Moon and when the Moon is in a barren or semi-barren fire or air sign such as Aries, Leo, Sagittarius, Libra, Gemini or Aquarius.

Moon Cords

One way of 'collecting' and keeping Moon energy is by making a Moon cord. The cord is made on a particular phase of the Moon and the energy is trapped in each knot and kept there until needed. So no matter what Moon phase it is, you always have the corresponding Moon energy to work your spell. Of course it is easier and better to do any working on the actual Moon phase, but sometimes it just isn't possible, so if you have Moon cords to hand you don't have to wait.

To make a Moon cord, use wool, string, cord or thread about 2 feet long. It helps if you have different colours then you can use a different colour for each phase of the Moon, to help identify them afterwards. You will need to be able to see and feel the Moon to make your cord. Here, the choice is yours – you can cast a full circle if you wish, otherwise I like to just light a candle and invoke a suitable lunar deity then ask them to lend their power. Face the Moon and hold your cord up towards it. You can say prepared words then, or just ask for what you need – the power of that particular phase of the Moon to be drawn down into your cord for safekeeping until you need it.

You can also use the following:

By knot of ONE, the spell's begun
By knot of TWO, it cometh true
By knot of THREE, so mote it be
By knot of FOUR, this power I store
By knot of FIVE, the spell's alive
By knot of SIX, this spell I fix
By knot of SEVEN, events I'll leaven
By knot of EIGHT, it will be Fate
By knot of NINE, what's done is mine

As you visualise the power entering your cord, start tying knots – you will need to tie nine in total, each an equal distance apart. If you don't use the chant above, on your last knot it is an idea to finish with 'so mote it be'.

Thank the deity and the Moon for their energies.

Keep the cord safe. When you need the energy from that particular Moon phase place it on your altar, around your candle or wherever you are working your spell.

There are two modes of thought on using the cord, you can either keep using it and just recharge it at the next Moon phase or you can actually undo one of the knots each time you need that energy to 'release' it, once you have used all the knots you can recharge it.

Moon Charms

You can make all sorts of charms to honour or work with lunar energies, including small bottles or medicine bags filled with herbs, crystals and oils that correspond to the Moon. Even a small shell or plain crystal to carry in your pocket if charged with the energy of the Moon works well.

Herbs and oils associated with the Moon:

Aloe: Protection and luck
Lemon balm: Love, success and healing
Bladder wrack: Protection, the sea, the wind, money, psychic powers
Cabbage: Luck
Camellia: Money and prosperity
Camphor: Health and divination
Chickweed: Fidelity and love
Clary sage: Protection, love and visions
Coconut: Protection and purification
Cotton: Luck, healing and protection
Cucumber: Healing and fertility
Eucalyptus: Healing and protection
Gardenia: Love, peace, healing and spirituality
Grape: Fertility, mental powers and money
Honeysuckle: Money, psychic powers and protection
Honesty: Money and protection
Jasmine: Love, money and dreams
Lemon: Purification, love and friendship
Lettuce: Protection, love, divination and sleep
Lily: Protection
Lotus: Protection
Mallow: Love, protection and exorcism
Melon: Healing, purification, love and changes

Moonwort: Money and love
Moss: Luck and money
Myrrh: Protection, exorcism, healing and spirituality
Passion flower: Peace, sleep and friendship
Peach: Love, exorcism, fertility and wishes
Poppy: Fertility, love, sleep, money and luck
Potato: Healing
Sandalwood: Protection, wishes, healing, exorcism and spirituality
Willow: Love, protection and healing

Crystals associated with the Moon:

Amethyst: Love, integrity, stress relief, healing, addictions, patience, peaceful sleep, psychic protection, psychic powers and restoring energy.

Angelite: Secrets, truth, compassion, peace, tranquillity, angel communication and heightened awareness.

Aquamarine: Travel, healing, cleansing, communication, intuition, psychic awareness, meditation and clairvoyance.

Azurite: Dreams, guidance, inner wisdom, psychic powers, healing, communication, visions and spiritual connections.

Beryl: Protection, sympathy, happiness and sincerity.

Blue calcite: Protection, negotiations, confidence, scrying, wishes and meditation.

Blue chalcedony: Rebirth, good fortune, protection, practicality, learning, stress, psychic communication and protection from psychic attack.

Blue lace agate: Motherhood, stress relief, energy, peace, clairaudience and divination.

Celestite: Meditation, balance, attunement, clarity, writing, communication, spiritual work, dreaming, harmony and hope.

Jade: Healing, good fortune, prosperity, friendship, repels negativity and dream work.

Lapis lazuli: Calming, contentment, loyalty, integrity, trust, night magic, psychic protection and dream work.

Lepidolite: Peaceful sleep, pain relief, messages, support, cleansing, psychic work, negativity.

Moonstone: Stone of the Moon Goddesses, healing, intuition, dreams, tension, peaceful sleep, protection for travellers, psychic abilities, divination and prophecy.

Mother of Pearl: Secrets, pregnancy, motherhood, prosperity, sea magic and wishes.

Opal: Transformation, self-worth, confidence, self-esteem, creativity, justice, protection, harmony, seduction, emotions and karma.

Pearl: Harmony, women's mysteries, spiritual love and romance.

Quartz: Health, wealth, happiness, optimism, all sorts of healing, cleansing, energising, harmony, absorbing negative energy and psychic powers.

Sapphire: Spiritual healing, channelling, loyalty, commitment, psychic powers, clairvoyance, clairaudience and prophecy.

Selenite: Named after the Moon Goddess Selene, enchantment, ritual, fertility, motherhood, partnerships, communication, dispelling fear and psychic communication.

Moon Crystal Amulet

You can use any crystal or tumble stone that you like for this, go with your intuition and pick one that resonates with you and makes you feel a connection to the Moon.

If possible do this outside under the Moon or in a window where the moonlight shines in. Sprinkle your chosen crystal with salt and then waft it through incense smoke to cleanse and purify it. After that very carefully pass the crystal over a candle flame and finally sprinkle it with Full Moon water.

Charge the crystal with your intent; it might be for protection, strength or courage, using the power of the moonlight.

Carry it with you in a small pouch, pocket or purse.

Moon Divination

The Full Moon, especially, is an excellent time to work with divination, as is the Dark Moon. The power of the Moon heightens your psychic senses. The Full Moon allows your creative and imaginative consciousness to surface, and the Dark Moon is a good time to reflect on your inner self.

I have mentioned a few ideas already within this book, but divination can be as simple as a bowl with a dark inside filled with water and set out so the moonlight shines into the water. You can also drop a silver coin into the bottom of the bowl to add to your reading, or sprinkle some herbs or drops of ink on the surface of the water to help create images.

Scrying is the art of seeing images or pictures in a surface, such as a bowl of water, a pond, a dark mirror or a crystal ball. Objects such as these are called speculums (which is Latin for the word mirror and not to be confused with the medical instrument of the same name!). The Elizabethan mathematician, astrologer and magician, John Dee, used many scrying devices including what he referred to as 'shew stones' – polished translucent or reflective objects, often made of obsidian that he used for his research.

Real crystal balls are incredibly expensive but I have had good results with smaller, cheaper glass globes. Set yourself up in a quiet place, I like to light a candle too. Ground and centre yourself and then gaze into the crystal, allowing your eyes to unfocus a little helps. Just let the images and shapes come to you.

A dark mirror is also an interesting speculum to use; these can be easily made by using a picture frame or old mirror and painting the back of the glass with black paint. Scry with your dark mirror in the same way you would a crystal ball.

Make sure you are relaxed and in a calm frame of mind, let yourself drift... Don't worry if you don't see much when you first try it, come away and try again later. Once you get the hang of it you will be able to ask specific questions. It helps to have a notebook handy to jot down any images or shapes you see; they might not make sense at the time but may do so later.

Dowsing is another form of divination that works well at the Full Moon. We normally associate the term dowsing with two hazel sticks used to find water or ley lines, but pendulums also fall under this category. There are many beautiful pendulums for sale in shops and on the internet, but they are also very easy to make. All you need is a piece of cord, string or chain and something fairly small but weighty to hang on the end of it – could be a stone with a hole in it, a shell, a small piece of wood or even a wedding ring!

You will also find that you don't always 'connect' with every type of pendulum, some will work with you, some won't, you will need to try them out to see. When you get or make a new pendulum it also helps to carry it with you for a while, and/or sleep with it under your pillow, just so that it attunes to your energies. It also helps to cleanse and charge your pendulum regularly by leaving it out in the moonlight, outside if you can do so safely, otherwise on a windowsill indoors is fine.

Start working with your pendulum by asking it simple questions such as 'give me a yes' and 'give me a no' so that you know which way it will swing to give you answers. Test it with questions so that you know how it works and how it will respond to you. Remember to keep your questions straight-forward and simple, don't confuse it!

I find it also helps to thank my pendulum once it has given me an answer; it stops it from swinging so that I can move onto the next question.

Faeries, Angels and Werewolves

Moon Faeries

How you see, hear and experience faeries is a very personal thing, but for me a Moon Faery is a very ethereal looking nature spirit. She, and I say she, as I have only ever met female Moon Faeries, is pale and beautiful, almost transparent sometimes. They are only ever seen at night and are extremely elusive. I do feel that seeing or meeting a Moon Faery brings good fortune your way.

Be careful though, as with all faeries they have a dark side and a Moon Faery can capture your gaze and hold it and you could become trapped within her gaze...

Moon Angels

There are lots of angelic beings associated with the Moon, in fact there are as many angels as there are days of the month nearly...

Angels associated with the moon include: Geniel, Enediel, Anixiel, Azariel, Gabriel, Dirachiel, Scheliel, Amnediel, Barbiel, Ardifiel, Neciel, Abdizuel, Jazeriel, Ergediel, Atliel, Azeruel, Adriel, Egibiel, Amutiel, Kyriel, Bethnael, Geliel, Requiel, Abrinael, Aziel, Tagriel, Atheniel and Amnixiel.

Werewolves

I had to put a piece in here about werewolves as they are always linked with the Moon. The official word for someone who turns into a wolf at the Full Moon is a lycanthrope. Back in medieval times if you were suspected of being a werewolf you were burnt to death. The legends suggest that the ways to become a lycanthrope are to be born a werewolf because of a curse that was placed upon you or your mother while she carried you, being a magician who could change willingly, or being bitten by another werewolf. There are also the legends that tell of Goddesses and

Gods that could shapeshift into wolves.

Hollywood, of course, has taken this legend and made a huge fortune out of it. It is a shame really that the wolf comes out of this legend in such a bad light, because in reality the wolf is a very intelligent and social animal!

I think the connection with the werewolf legend is possibly one of transformation within, the Full Moon power being as strong as it is being the prompt for such a transition, the werewolf being the naked, raw animal part of our psyche... or perhaps werewolves really do exist...

Moon Crafts

Making a Moon Candle

If you are very crafty making your own candles is fun, but messy! Craft shops do sell pretty good candle making kits as well. However, you can always buy a readymade candle and decorate it yourself.

For a Moon Candle I would go with white to represent the Moon or you could tailor the colour to the Moon phase of white for waxing, red for full or black for waning, it is your choice.

Pillar candles are ideal for decorating as it gives you a bit more space to work. You can paint lunar images on the outside, stick crescent Moon shapes on it, tie ribbons around it, dress it with an oil Moon blend and roll it in crushed herbs or inscribe Moon symbols into the wax – be creative!

Moon Hanger

You can purchase wire circles in craft shops or if you are very patient and strong you can cut up a wire coat hanger and bend it into a circle shape. Cover your circle with ribbon by winding it around. Then tie three lengths of silver ribbon or cord equally around the circle so that they hang down. Then add whatever symbols, beads or bits and bobs you want to. Shells would be good as they have a connection to the Moon, sparkly crystals or small mirror pieces work well or cut out images from silver card, maybe in the shapes of your Moon animal totem or stick with crescent Moon shapes.

The Moon Tarot Card

One of the major arcana tarot cards is The Moon; you can use this card on your Moon altar or within spell workings, although you may have your own meanings for the Moon card, here are some of my thoughts on what it means:

- Illusion, underworld, emotions
- Something is blocking your light
- Pass through the gateway for the answers
- Veils of illusion, mysterious
- Struggle with the conscious
- Temptations, be careful
- Thresholds
- Superstition
- Deal with the areas of your life that need attention to find clarity and answers
- Threshold of a new experience or period in life
- Sometimes we have to look at the darker aspects of our personality to understand and move forward
- Listen and look for guidance
- You may have to deal with some uncomfortable home truths, it may not be what you want to see but it is necessary
- Are you ignoring or refusing to see something?
- This card totally says illusion and mystery to me, and dealing with the shadow self.

Moon Tarot Card Spell – Knowledge

This spell is to tap into your subconscious for knowledge.

You will need:

Three tarot cards – The Moon, The High Priestess and The Hermit.

Lay out the cards in order from left to right. Firstly sit quietly and look at The Moon card, study it in detail, really seeing all the images, and think about its connection to your subconscious, your imagination, inspiration, dreams and intuition. Then move onto The High Priestess, think of your desire to seek knowledge and wisdom, perhaps to have insight into a mystery. Lastly look at The Hermit card, see the image as yourself holding a lantern up high to shine light onto the unknown, to illuminate the knowledge that you seek.

When you have finished with the visualisation, light a candle (blue or purple would work well but go with a colour that you are drawn to). Watch the flame of the candle and ask the Divine to grant you access to the hidden knowledge that you want to find. Sit for as long as you can watching the candle flame and meditating on the three tarot cards. When you are ready, snuff the candle. Watch out for signs and symbols as you go about your day, or if performing this spell in the evening take note of your dreams.

Moon Tarot Card Spell – Guilt

This spell uses The Moon tarot card to get rid of negative emotions and old guilt that tends to hang around making a nuisance of itself.

You will need:
Three tarot cards, the Moon, Judgement and The World
A white candle
A piece of paper and a pen
A cauldron or fire-proof dish

Make yourself comfortable and make sure you have all the items to hand.

Light the white candle then, sitting in front of the candle as it burns, write down on the piece of paper all the emotions and issues that have been causing you unrest, all the old guilt issues and negative thoughts. Take as much time as you need.

Then lay The Moon card down. As you do so think about all the words that you have written down, think how much pain they cause you and how heavy they make your energy. Come to the realisation that you must let go of these energies, you cannot change what happened in the past, and the negative energies you have created serve you no good.

As you feel the need to release these negative energies, screw the piece of paper with your list up in your hand then catch it on fire in the candle flame, dropping it into the cauldron and allowing it to burn.

As you watch the paper burning, lay down The Judgement card. See this card as your transformation, your rebirth. Call upon the power of the candle flame to purify you. The power of fire can cleanse, release and restore.

Then lay The World card down. This card represents you taking back your own power, replacing the negative energy with positive. You are refreshed, renewed and transformed.

When you are ready, snuff the candle out and bury any leftover stub along with the ashes of the paper in the earth.

And finally...

She is so powerful and so wonderful – once you start working with the Moon and her phases a whole new way of thinking and working magic will open up to you...

Bibliography

Cunningham's Encyclopaedia of Magical Herbs by Scott Cunningham

A Complete Guide to Night Magic by Cassandra Eason

Healing Crystals by Cassandra Eason

Advanced Witchcraft by Edain McCoy

Solitary Witch by Silver Raven Wolf

Power of the Moon by Teresa Moorey

Moon Magic by DJ Conway

Tarot Spells by Janina Renee

MOON
BOOKS

Moon Books invites you to begin or deepen your encounter with Paganism, in all its rich, creative, flourishing forms.